SWEET TENNESSEE HYMNS

SMOKY MOUNTAIN FAVORITES FOR ACOUSTIC GUITAR SOLO

by Gerard Garno

Dedication
To Chet Atkins and Rick Foster, the guitarists who inspired this book.

A cassette tape and compact disc of the music in this book are now available. The publisher strongly recommends the use of one of these recordings along with the text to insure accuracy of interpretation and ease in learning.

ABOUT THE AUTHOR

Gerard Joseph Garno is the first-prize winner of the 1981 Society of American Musicians National Competition, a prize winner in the 1983 Music Teachers National Association Competition, first-prize winner of the 1984 Society of American Musicians National Competition, first-prize winner of the 1986 American String Teachers Association National Competition, and was a finalist in the 1987 Toronto International Guitar Competition (after competing with almost 90 other guitarists from around the world).

Gerard started guitar studies at age 11 with Larry Williams, and later began study of the classic guitar with Ken Hummer. He did his undergraduate degree work at the Chicago Musical College under Pamela Kimmel, and at the Cincinnati Conservatory of Music under Clare Callahan, where he graduated magna cum laude. He has studied in master classes with Oscar Ghiglia, Christopher Parkening, Elliot Fisk, Robert Guthrie, John Holmquist, Leo Brouwer, George Sakellariou, David Russell, Manuel Barrueco, and Carlos Barbosa-Lima.

Gerard comes from a farm family of fifteen children, born and raised outside of Adrian, Michigan. After beginning a serious study of the guitar at age 11, Gerard began to achieve success in rock music. By age 15, he was playing professionally, and was deeply engrossed in the rock culture and the sinful life-style that goes along with it. While successful in the eyes of the world, Gerard found this life-style to be empty and meaningless. At the age of 16, Gerard came to know Jesus Christ as his personal Lord and Savior, completely turning from his former way of life, and experiencing the true joy and fulfillment of the Christian life. Since that time, Gerard has been striving to glorify God with his musical talent and Christian testimony. Gerard is a staff member with the music ministry of Campus Crusade for Christ.

A virtuoso performer, Gerard Garno has developed a special interdenominational ministry, playing instrumental Christian and classical music on solo guitar. His ministry includes playing full concerts and special music for worship services, as well as sharing music and testimony for youth functions and all types of Christian gatherings. Gerard also performs on both television and radio, and has made several recordings which serve to partially support his ministry.

"Gerard Garno's music springs from a deep Christian commitment, a gifted young player." (Christopher Parkening)

"A wonderful contribution to the Praise Gathering . . . we heard wonderful comments about the weekend." (Bill Gaither)

". . . excellent technique and music sincerity . . . will bring much joy to those who listen." (Rick Foster)

"A solid technique, very musical . . . precise and professional . . ." (Toledo Blade)

"A very talented artist and a real musician's musician." (Greg Buchanan)

"I play some guitar, but Gerard is a *real* guitar player . . . " (Steve Green)

"Gerard Garno is good, he is really good!" (Dino Kartsonakis)

"A great player with a good heart." (Gary McSpadden)

"You couldn't play the guitar any better . . ." (Larnelle Harris)

"Gerard has a strong and polished technique . . . fine musicality . . . great potential . . ." (Liona Boyd)

For information regarding recordings and/or concert bookings contact:

Gerard Garno
26 Saint Lawrence Street W.
Box 460 - Suite 7960
Madoc, Ontario
Canada K0K 2K0

Gerard Garno

ACKNOWLEDGMENTS

I want to express my gratitude to those who have made this book possible:

To John Basford, who spent hours going through his record collection to help me find the right songs and arrangements.

To all the talented arrangers whose work helped to make this book complete.

To Chet Atkins, the king of the Tennessee guitar style. While I have only met Chet once, I have admired him from afar. The tremendous impact of his work can be seen by the fact that every arrangement in this book is based on his style, even though the arrangers that contributed are of very different ages and from different geographical locations.

To Rick Foster, one of the first to use the acoustic classic guitar to play hymns. Rick has become a great encouragement and inspiration to me as well as many other guitarists. I have enjoyed sharing arrangements with him over the last few years. I greatly appreciate having his permission to use some of his arrangements for this book.

To all my fellow Christians in the Baptist Church, particularly the Southern Baptist Church. It was your love for this style of music that inspired me to do this project!

To Ernie Smith, who sent several arrangements to me as soon as he heard of this project. I feel that his work is some of the best in this book.

To Bill Bay, for catching the vision for this book. It is an honor to work with his great company.

To Jesus Christ, my best friend.

To my wife Laura, for designing the cover, editing some of the manuscript, and most of all for her love and support.

CONTENTS

PREFACE

I am excited to be able to offer this book of *Sweet Tennessee Hymns*. This book corresponds to my ninth recording by that same title. This is the first project that I have done using mostly American hymns done in the Tennessee style made popular by guitarists such as Chet Atkins and Merle Travis. I had focused for many years on playing hymns of European origin in a classical style. It's not that I didn't like other styles, but rather, the classical approach reflected my several years of conservatory training and my liturgical church background. (Country music was not taught at the conservatory!)

After graduating from the Cincinnati Conservatory in 1988, I began playing concerts in churches full-time, and found that with the exception of some high church settings, most churches were requesting the kind of hymn tunes and arrangements contained in this book. I believe that the reason this music is so popular is that it is music with a unique place in American history and culture. For example, "Amazing Grace" is a traditional American tune that was set to the words of John Newton, a slave trader turned Christian. "There is a Fountain" originated in the Western part of America as a camp meeting song. "Battle Hymn of the Republic" is one of America's most cherished songs from the Civil War era. Each one of these hymns has a unique story. These are songs that speak from the heart to touch and inspire millions. It is my prayer that this book of *Sweet Tennessee Hymns* will help to keep the message of these great songs alive, and will be enjoyed by guitarists everywhere!

Gerard Garno
Cincinnati, OH
1993

INTRODUCTION

In recent years there has been a great deal of interest in the Smoky Mountain or Tennessee-flavored style of music. Several recordings of that style have been released. All this has sparked my interest in doing a recording for solo guitar, and a corresponding book so the music could be shared with other guitarists. I spent many hours working to make a book that would be usable by guitarists of all levels and playing styles. Each hymn is presented in the following ways:

1. Simple fingerstyle arrangement.

I have created this arrangement to be playable by less advanced guitarists. It stays in the lower positions and avoids complicated passages. While this arrangement is simple, I have incorporated beautiful harmonies with correct voice leading so it would be suitable for performance. This is also included in tablature for guitarists who don't read music. (an explaination of the tablature is included on page 11.)

2. Advanced fingerstyle arrangement.

This arrangement corresponds to the recording I made of *Sweet Tennessee Hymns*. It makes no compromise in the area of technique and is suitable for concerts, church services, etc. It is also included in tablature.

3. Hymn texts and tunes with chords.

Study of the text is important for grasping the spirit of each hymn and is highly recommended. This presentation will also be helpful to guitarists who want to accompany individual or group singing. Or, it may be used as a duet with one guitar playing the melody line and the other playing the chords. More advanced guitarists may find it helpful to play this version in order to get more familiar with the melody line and the harmonies of each hymn.

I have used chord graphs that show the exact fingering of each chord. I realize that the use of bars and the fourth finger may be uncomfortable to some guitarists, so I have indicated which chords may have an alternate fingering. The alternate chords are given at the end of each hymn tune. Each chord graph also uses an "x" to show which strings are *not* to be played while strumming or plucking the chord.

A cassette or CD of *Sweet Tennessee Hymns* is available through Mel Bay Publications. This recording could be very helpful for learning these arrangements, and especially in regard to musical interpretation.

Eight other solo guitar recordings are available. (Ten dollars for cassettes, fifteen dollars for CDs, and one dollar for postage and handling charges. Please enclose a check with your order payable to Gerard Garno and send to the address listed on page 4.)

1. *A Guitar for the Holidays* (cassette or CD).
   An hour-long recording of Christmas music.

2. *Lazy Lullaby Music* (cassette only).
   A relaxing recording of children songs and worship choruses.

3. *Psalms, Hymns and Spiritual Songs, Vol. 1* (cassette only).
   A recording of hymns, contemporary Christian music and praise choruses.

4. *Psalms, Hymns, and Spiritual Songs, Vol. 2* (cassette only).
   A recording of traditional hymns and sacred classical music.

5. *A Musical Offering* (cassette only).
   An hour-long recording of classical music.

6. *Meditation with The Master* (cassette only).
   Eighty minutes of reflective music including hymns, choruses, and original music.

7. *Guitar Praise and Hymnspiration* (cassette only).
   A virtuosic Spanish/jazz flavored recording of praise songs and hymns.

8. *MasterPieces* (cassette only).
   Contemporary and traditional Christian music done in a virtuosic classical style.

HOW TO READ TABLATURE

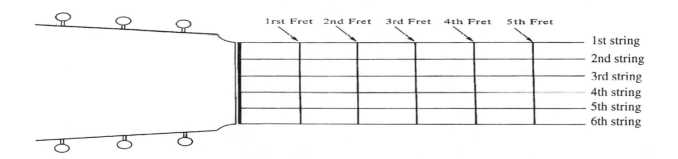

In tablature the lines represent strings. The numbers on the lines indicate frets (0 = open string). In the following example a C chord would be played: (1st string open; 2nd string press down on the 1st fret; 3rd string open; 4th string press down on the 2nd fret; 5th string press down on the 3rd fret; finally, do not play the 6th string.)

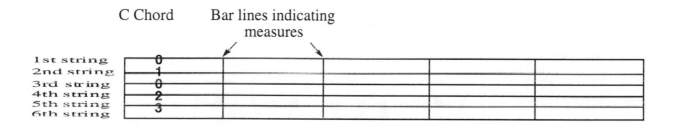

I'LL FLY AWAY

This is probably the most famous hymn written by Albert Brumley. It has been recorded more than five hundred times by various artists of many styles of music. The first publishing was in 1933 as the number eighteen song in Hartford's hymnal, *The Wonderful Message*. The first known recording was by evangelist Rex Humbard and his family for the American Recording Company in April 1940. It was released on the Vocalion label. The arrangement featured Humbard and his wife singing the song as an up-tempo duet with guitar and mandolin accompaniment.

Brumley first felt the inspiration for this song as he worked in an Oklahoma cotton field. He derived it from the opening line of an old Vernon Dalhart record called *The Prisoner's Song*. Its famous opening line was "If I had the wings of an angel...."

I have arranged the first fingerstyle arrangement in a straightforward manner over an alternating bass line. The advanced arrangement was done by Ernie Smith and is a great masterpiece. It features a dynamic walking country bass line and a snappy rhythm. Ernie first started listening to this song after it was recorded by the Chuck Wagon Gang in December 1948 for Columbia. He got the idea of using the walking bass line from one of Rick Foster's arrangements, and found that it worked splendidly with this hymn. Rick Foster first recorded this arrangement on his *Sacred Classic Guitar* album.

Melody-only version: Page 19

I'LL FLY AWAY

Arranged for
the guitar by
Gerard Garno

by Albert E.
Brumley

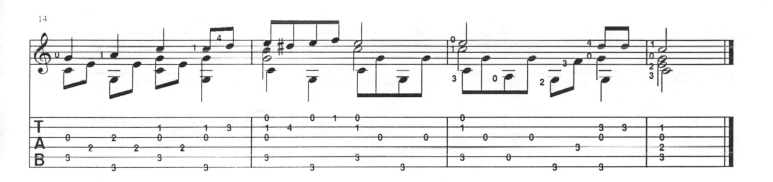

I'LL FLY AWAY

Arranged for the guitar by
Ernie Smith

by Albert E. Brumley

I'LL FLY AWAY

Arranged for the guitar
by Gerard Garno

Words and Music
by Albert E. Brumley

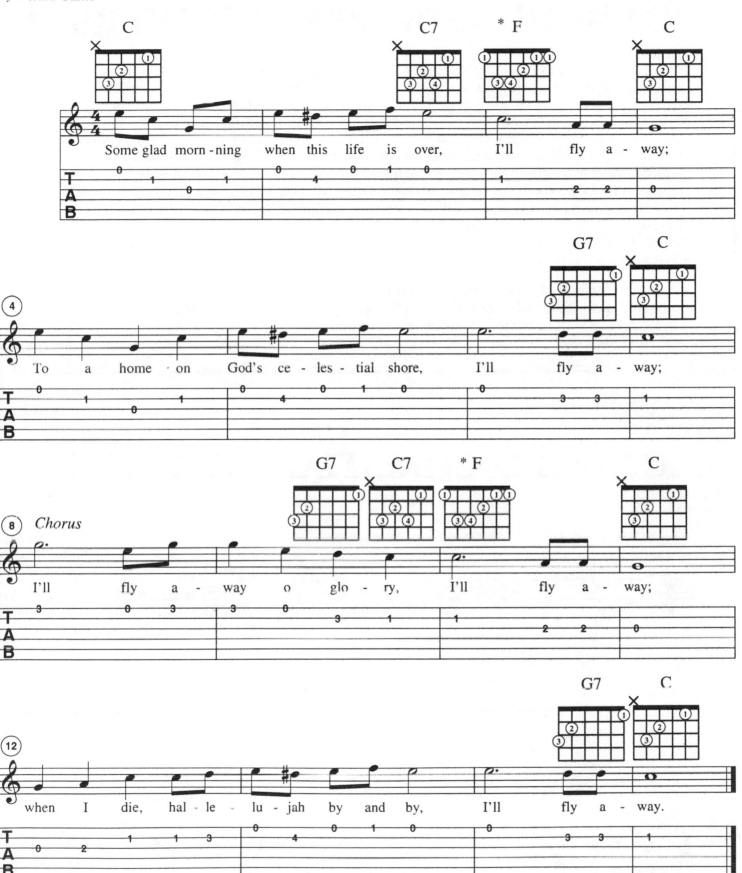

2. When the shadows of this life have grown,
   I'll fly away;
   Like a bird from prison bars has flown,
   I'll fly away.
   Chorus

3. Just a few more weary days and then,
   I'll fly away;
   To a land where joy shall never and,
   I'll fly away.
   Chorus

* F

19

ONWARD CHRISTIAN SOLDIERS

This hymn was written in 1864 by writer and Anglican minister, Sabine Baring-Gould in Yorkshire, England. A children's festival was to be held in which the children would march from village to village carrying a cross and banners. Baring-Gould wanted something for the children to sing as they marched. He couldn't find anything that he felt was suitable, so he sat up one night and hastily wrote this hymn. He wrote it simply without any thought of publication, and remarked years later that nothing surprised him more than its popularity. The hymn was first sung to the tune of Haydn's "Symphony in D." Arthur Sullivan wrote the tune that is now used in 1871 for inclusion in his hymnal called *Hymnary.* The current version of this hymn was published in America by the Methodist-Episcopal Book Room in Philadelphia in an 1873 hymnal by John R. Sweeney called *Gems of Praise.* It is interesting to note that some contemporary liberal denominations have discussed removing this hymn from their hymnals because it mentions war.

I was first inspired to arrange this hymn for guitar when I heard it played by an anonymous guitarist on an old Tennessee sampler album. Strict attention should be paid to the march rhythm that characterizes this hymn.

Melody-only version: Page 29

ONWARD CHRISTIAN SOLDIERS

Arranged for
the guitar by
Gerard Garno

by Arthur Sullivan

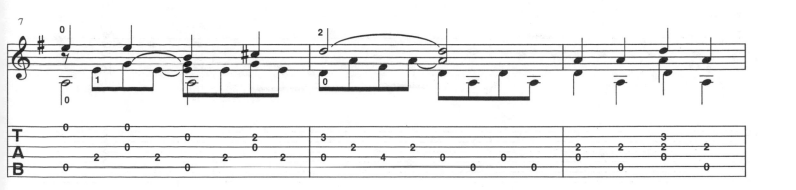

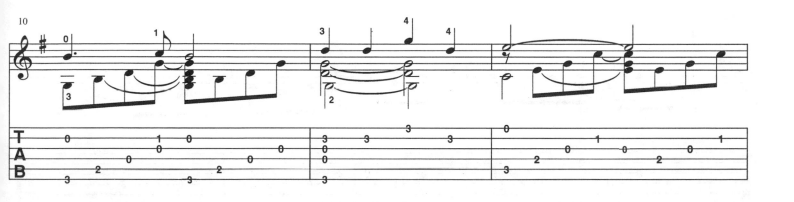

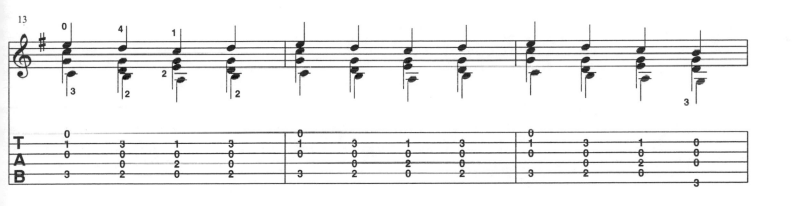

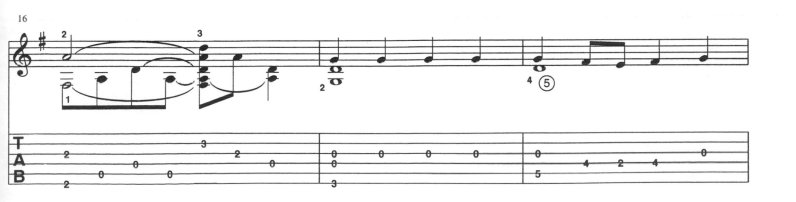

22

ONWARD CHRISTIAN SOLDIERS

Adapted and
arranged for
the guitar
by Gerard Garno

by Arthur Sullivan

23

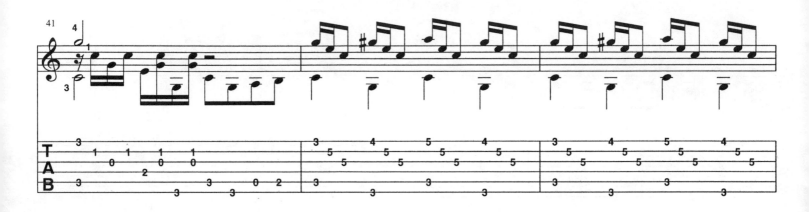

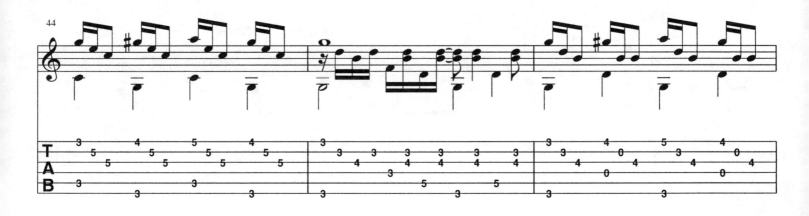

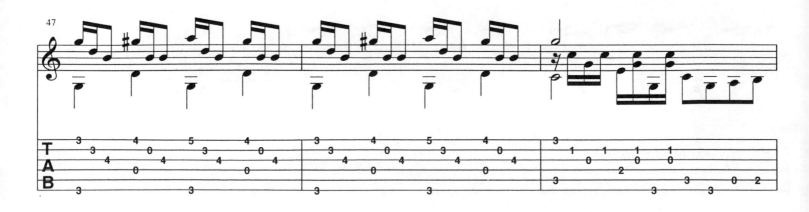

strums

28

ONWARD CHRISTIAN SOLDIERS

Arranged for the guitar
by Gerard Garno

Music by Arthur Sullivan
Words by Sabine Baring-Gould

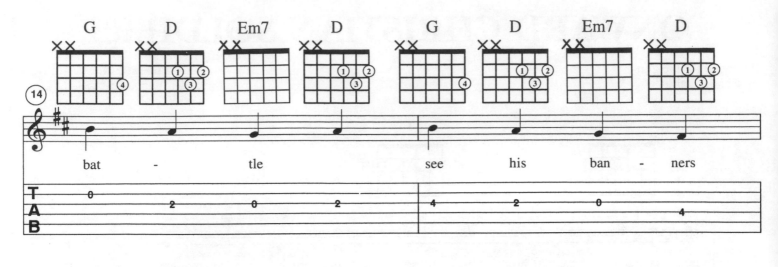

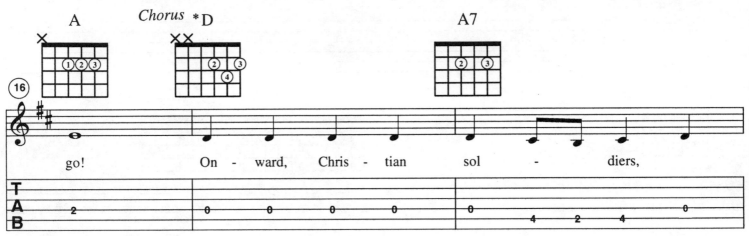

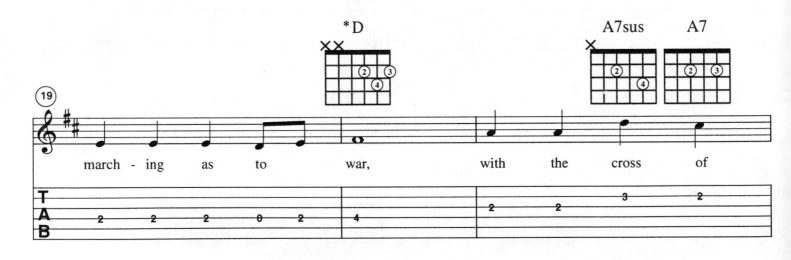

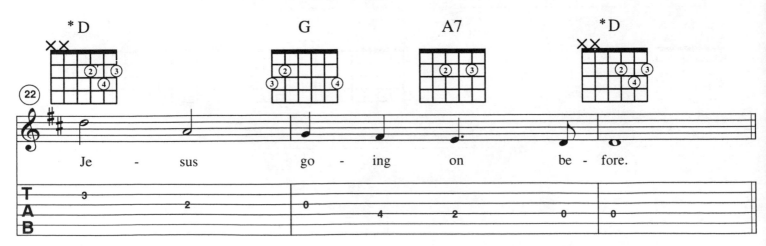

2. At the sign of triumph Satan's host doth flee;
On then, Christian soldiers, on to victory!
Hell's foundations quiver at the shout of praise;
Brothers, lift your voices, loud your anthems raise.
Chorus

3. Like a mighty army moves the church of God;
Brothers, we are treading where the saints have trod.
We are not divided, all one body we,
One in hope and doctrine, one in charity.
Chorus

4. Crowns and thrones may perish, kingdoms rise and wane,
But the church of Jesus constant will remain.
Gates of hell can never against that church prevail;
We have Christ's own promise, and that cannot fail.
Chorus

5. Onward then ye people, join our happy throng,
Blend with ours your voices in the triumph song.
Glory, laud and honor unto Christ the King,
This through countless ages men and angels sing.
Chorus

*D

THE OLD RUGGED CROSS

This hymn was written by George Bennard, a Methodist Episcopal minister, in 1913. It has become one of the most popular of all twentieth century hymns. Bennard wrote this hymn as he was meditating and praying about the centrality of the cross of Christ to the Christian faith. Inspiration for this hymn first came to him as he was holding evangelistic crusades in Albion, Michigan. Bennard spent the last years of his life near Reed City, Michigan, where a twelve-foot high cross was erected near his home. On it were engraved the words, "The Old Rugged Cross–Home of George Bennard, composer of this beloved hymn."

I had never been satisfied with other fingerstyle guitar arrangements of this hymn, so I decided to do my own. I did these arrangements intending them to be played freely with great emotion. The notes should be allowed to ring where indicated, and at times there should be an improvisatory feel.

Melody-only version: Page 40

THE OLD RUGGED CROSS

Arranged for the
guitar by Gerard Garno

by George Bennard

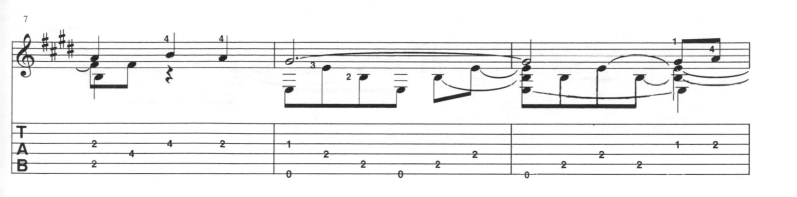

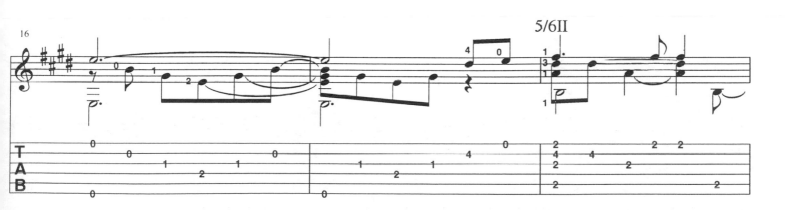

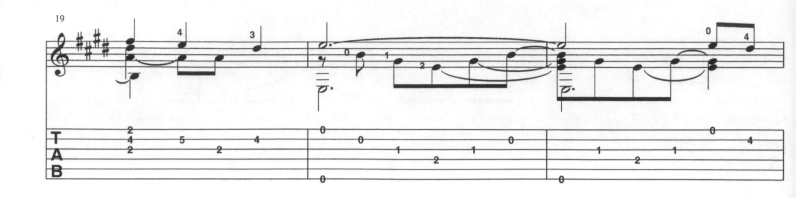

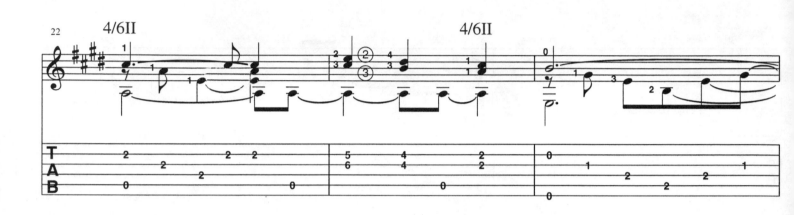

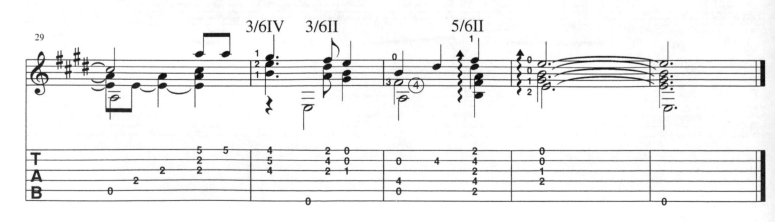

THE OLD RUGGED CROSS

Arranged for the guitar
by Gerard Garno

by George Bennard

THE OLD RUGGED CROSS

Arranged for the
guitar by Gerard Garno

by George Bennard

40

Chorus

So I'll cher - ish the old rug - ged cross

till my tro - phies at last I lay down;

I will cling to the old rug - ged cross,

and ex - chang it some day for a crown.

2. O that old rugged cross, so despised by the world,
Gas a wonderous attraction for me.
For the dear lamb of God left His glory above,
To bear it to dark Calvary.
Chorus

3. In the old rugged cross, stained with blood so divine,
A wondrous beauty I see;
For t'was on that old cross Jesus suffered and died,
To pardon and sanctify me.
Chorus

4. To the old rugged cross I will ever be true,
It's shame and reproach gladly bear;
Then He'll call me someday to my home far away,
Where His glory forever I'll share.
Chorus

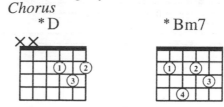

VICTORY IN JESUS

In 1939, E. M. Bartlett wrote the words and music to this hymn in Hartford, Arkansas. That same year it was published in James D. Vaughn's hymnal called *Gospel Choruses*. Bartlett initially copyrighted the song in his own name, but later sold the copyright to the Stamps-Baxter Music Company in Dallas, Texas. Before his death in 1941, he signed a renewal to Albert Brumley and Sons in Powell, Missouri. That renewal became effective in 1967.

This hymn has become a great favorite, and almost a theme song in the Baptist church. I heard gospel pianist Dino Kartsonakis playing an arrangement of it some time ago. His playing inspired me to arrange it for the guitar. These arrangements should be played with a light and happy feel. In order to play them smoothly, make sure to follow the barring instructions precisely. (For example, in measure 3 of the simple fingerstyle arrangement I indicate a first-position bar to be put in place before the fourth beat of that measure, not before the first beat of the next measure.)

Melody-only version: Page 49

VICTORY IN JESUS

Arranged for the guitar
by Gerard Garno

by E.M. Bartlett

III

VICTORY IN JESUS

Arranged for the guitar
by Gerard Garno

by E. M. Bartlett

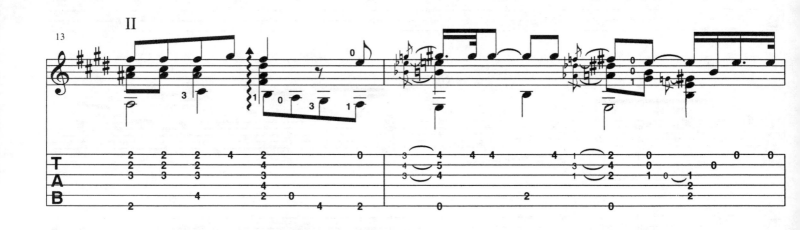

VICTORY IN JESUS

Arranged for the guitar
by Gerard Garno

Words and Music by
E.M.Bartlett

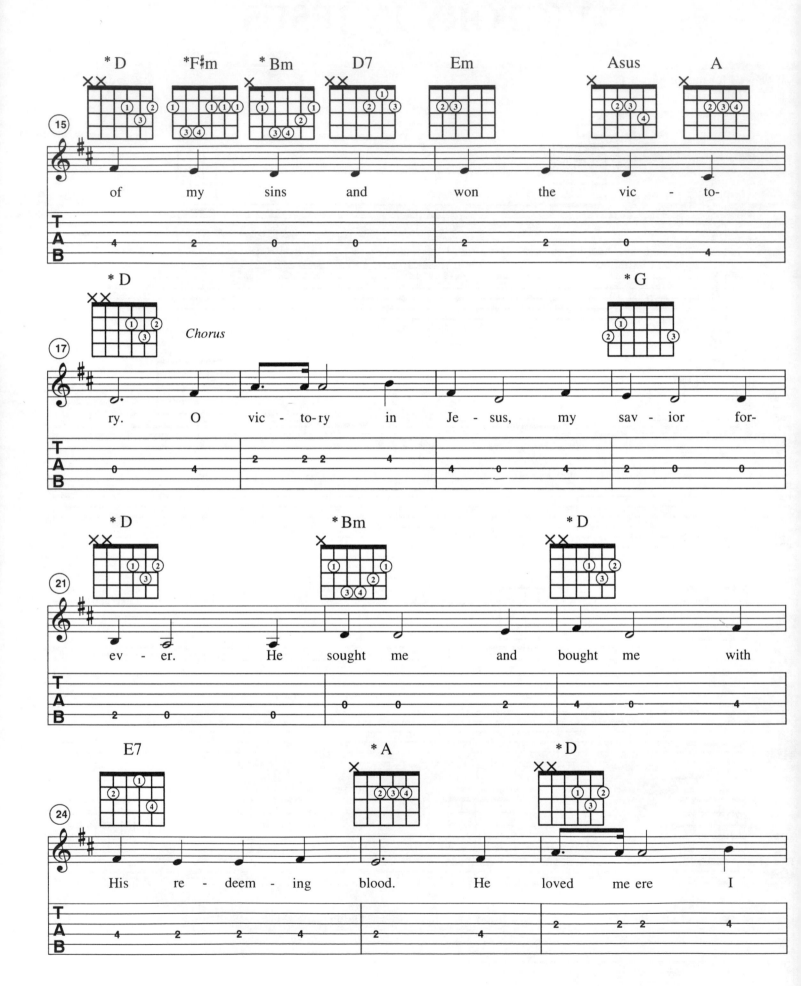

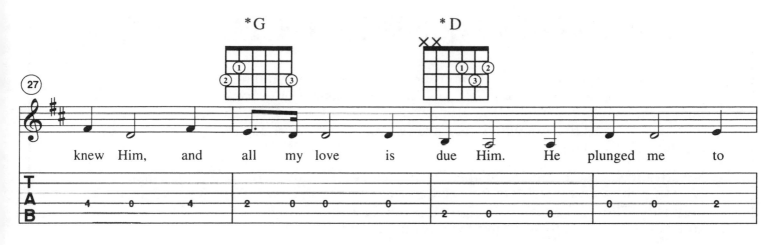

*G *D

knew Him,   and   all   my love   is   due Him.   He   plunged me   to

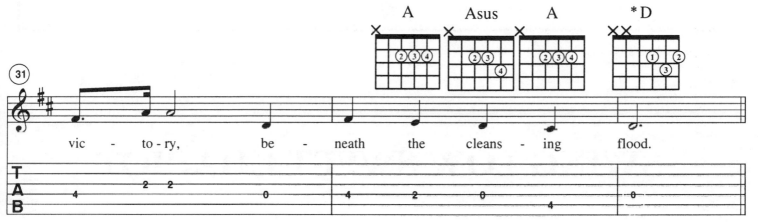

A   Asus   A   *D

vic - to - ry,   be - neath   the   cleans - ing   flood.

2. I heard about the healing, of His cleansing power revealing.
How He made the lame to walk again and caused the blind to see.
And then I cried "Dear Jesus, come and heal my broken spirit,"
And somehow Jesus came and brought to me the victory.
Chorus

3. I heard about a mansion He has built for me in glory.
And I heard about the streets of gold beyond the crystal sea.
About the angels singing, and the old redeemtion story,
And some sweet day I'll sing up there the song of victory.
Chorus

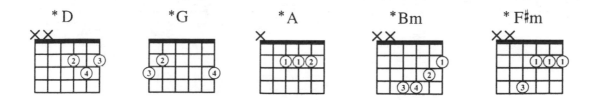

*D   *G   *A   *Bm   * F♯m

SWING LOW SWEET CHARIOT

While a specific writer for this hymn is not known, it is known that it originated as a popular Negro spiritual. It originated in America sometime prior to the Civil War. Most of the black population at that time was in bondage to a form of slavery based on race. Spirituals such as this one lifted the slave's spirits as they worked, and gave them hope of a better life to come.

My advanced arrangement is adapted from Rick Foster's book *Hymns for the Classic Guitar*, published by Mel Bay Publications. Rick Foster and Mark Casstevens arranged it originally. They did a marvelous job of capturing a soulish rhythmic mood. I have revised and modified it slightly to fit my own technique and playing style.

Melody-only version: Page 59

SWING LOW SWEET CHARIOT

Arranged for the
guitar by Gerard Garno

Traditional Afro -
American Spiritual

SWING LOW SWEET CHARIOT

Arranged for the guitar by
Rick Foster
and Gerard Garno

Traditional
Afro-American Spiritual

57

SWING LOW SWEET CHARIOT

Arranged for the guitar
by Gererd Garno

Traditional Afro-American Spiritual

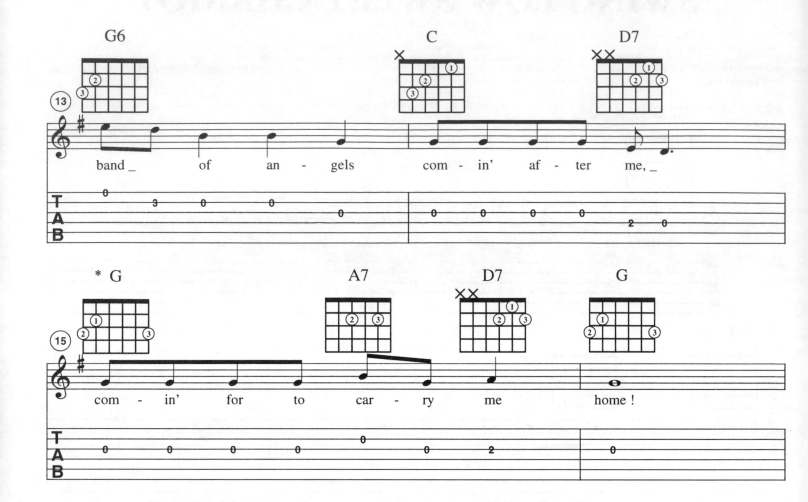

band __ of an - gels com - in' af - ter me, __ com - in' for to car - ry me home !

*G

2. *Chorus*
   If you get there before I do ,
   Comin' for to carry me home;
   Tell all my friends I'm coming too,
   Comin' for to carry me home.

3. *Chorus*
   I'm sometimes up, I'm sometimes down,
   Comin' for to carry me home.
   But still my soul feels heavenly bound,
   Comin' for to carry me home.

4. *Chorus*
   The brightest day that I can say,
   Comin' for to carry me home;
   When Jesus washed my sins away,
   Comin' for to carry me home.

THERE IS A FOUNTAIN

The writer, William Cowper, is believed to have written this hymn in 1771. It first appeared in a hymnal by Conyer called *Collection of Psalms and Hymns* in 1772.

Cowper was born into an English family of royalty from his mother's side. His father was a minister. Cowper was always known to be a frail child and a bit emotionally unstable. His mother died when he was six, further weakening his stability. Cowper studied law but suffered a mental breakdown prior to his bar examination. He then attempted suicide and was placed in an insane asylum for eighteen months. During his detention Cowper studied the Bible and was converted to Christianity when he found the forgiveness of Christ. He later wrote "There is a Fountain" based on the Old Testament text, Zechariah 13:1, "In that day there shall be a fountain opened to the house of David and to the inhabitants of Jerusalem for sin and uncleanness." The tune that was set to this text is a traditional American campmeeting tune from the early nineteenth century.

I was inspired to arrange this hymn when I saw an arrangement of it in Mel Bay's *Anthology of Beloved Hymns for Guitar*. I tried to reflect the tragic yet joyful subject matter of this hymn text in my advanced arrangement.

Melody-only version: Page 66

THERE IS A FOUNTAIN

Arranged for the guitar
by Gerard Garno

Traditional American melody

THERE IS A FOUNTAIN

Arranged for the guitar
by Gerard Garno

Traditional
American Tune

THERE IS A FOUNTAIN

Arranged for the guitar
by Gerard Garno

Words by William Cowper
Traditional American melody

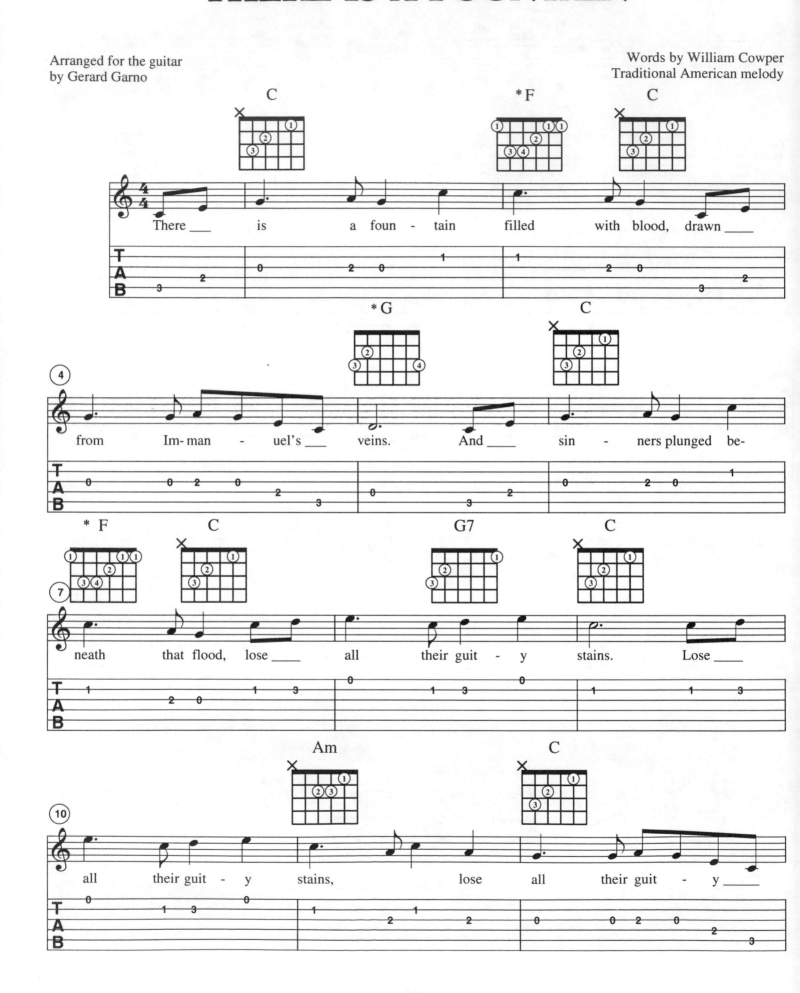

66

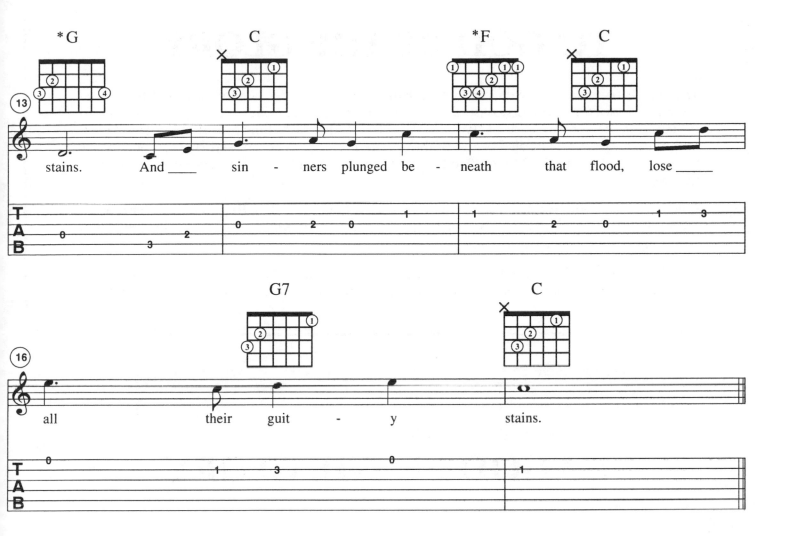

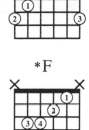

2. The dying thief rejoiced to see that fountain in his day.
And there may I, tho' vile as he, wash all my sins away.
Wash all my sins away, wash all my sins away.
And there may I, tho, vile as he, wash all my sins away.

3. E'er since by faith I saw the stream. Thy flowing wounds supply,
Redeeming love has been my theme, and shall be till I die.
And shall be till I die, and shall be till I die.
Redeeming love has been my theme and shall be till I die.

4. Then in a nobler, sweeter song I'll sing thy power to save.
When this poor lisping, stamm'ring tounge, lies silent in the grave.
Lies silent in the grave, lies silent in the grave.
When this poor lisping, stamm'ring tounge, lies silent in the grave.

TO GOD BE THE GLORY

The words to this hymn were written by Fanny Crosby. Fanny became blind at the age of six when a doctor applied hot poultices to her inflamed eyes. She went on to become a brilliant teacher in New York City. She wrote thousands of hymns and humbly refused to take much money or credit for any of them. The music was composed by New Jersey businessman William H. Doane. He frequently worked with Fanny to provide tunes for her texts.

This hymn was first published in a Sunday school hymnal called *Brightest and Best* in 1875. However, it was largely forgotten in America until it was reintroduced by the Billy Graham evangelistic team in 1954.

This hymn should be played with a bright and joyful feel. My advanced arrangement is a very demanding variation piece that was inspired by the arranging style of Ernie Smith.

Melody-only version: Page 83

TO GOD BE THE GLORY

Arranged for the guitar by
Gerard Garno

by William H. Doane

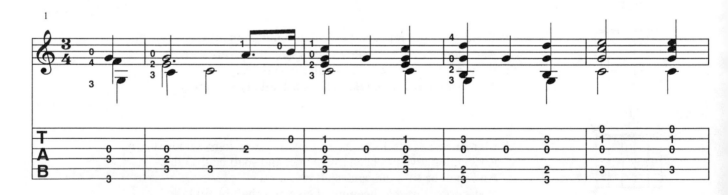

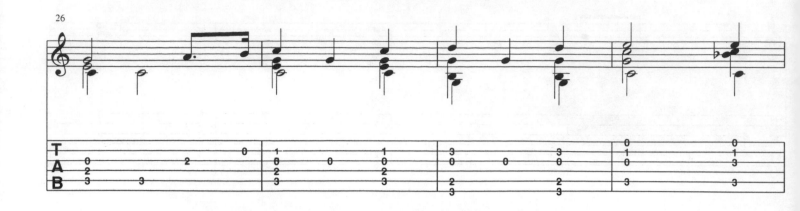

TO GOD BE THE GLORY

Arranged for the guitar by
Gerard Garno

by William H. Doane

muted with the thumb

TO GOD BE THE GLORY

Arranged for the guitar
by Gerard Garno

Words by Fanny J. Crosby
Music by William H. Doane

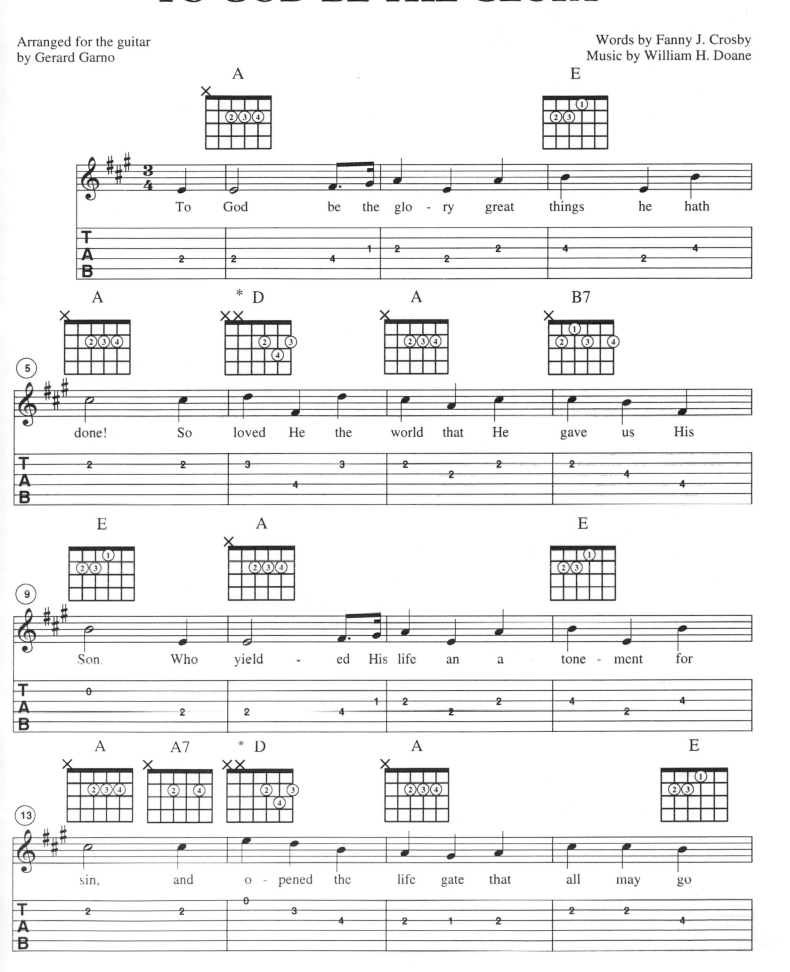

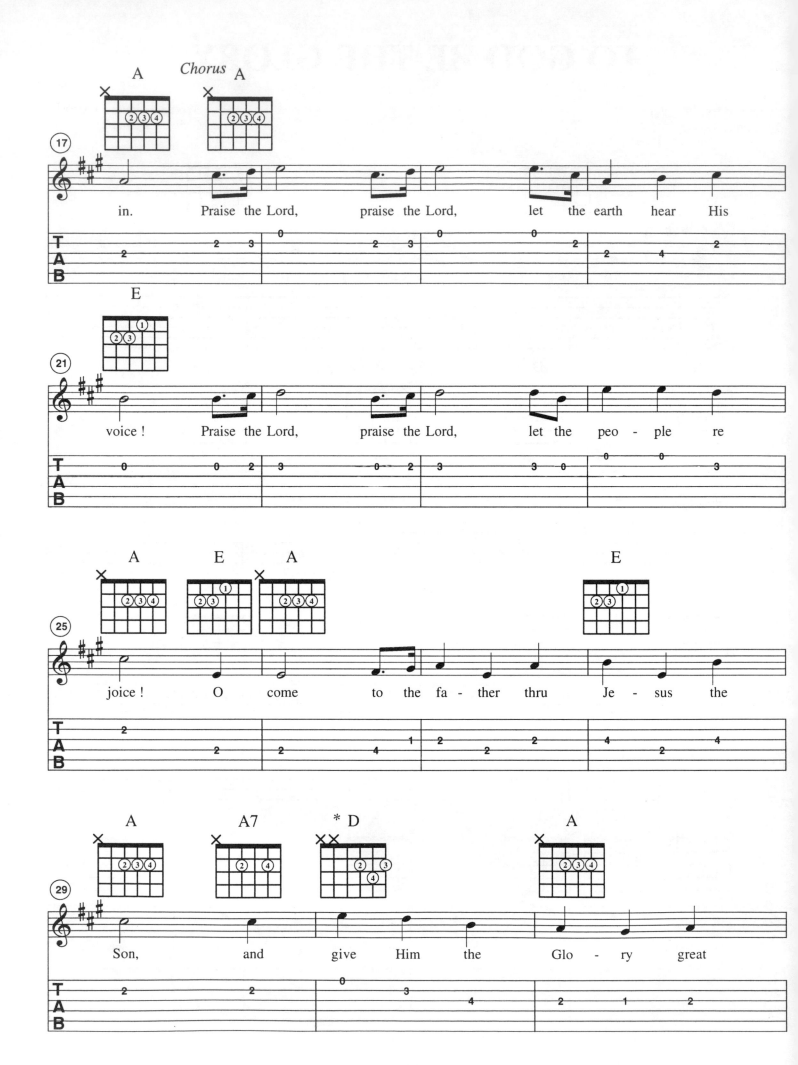

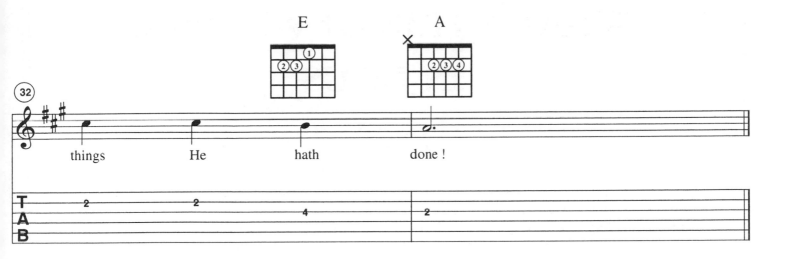

things   He   hath   done !

2. O perfect redemption, the purchase of blood,
   To every believer the promise of God.
   The vilest offender who truly believes,
   That moment from Jesus a pardon receives.
   Chorus

3. Great things He hath taught us, great things He hath done,
   And great our rejoicing thru Jesus the Son.
   But purer, and higher, and greater will be,
   Our wonder, our transport, when Jesus we see.
   Chorus

*D

WHAT A FRIEND WE HAVE IN JESUS

This beautiful hymn text was written by Joseph Scriven in 1855, to give comfort to his mother while she was in a time of sorrow. He never intended it to be published.

Scriven was born into a prosperous family in Dublin, Ireland. At the age of twenty-five he moved to Canada where he lived for the rest of his life. Two great tragedies kept him from ever marrying and greatly impacted his life. In his early days in Ireland his bride-to-be was accidentally drowned the night before their wedding. Then, while he was in Canada he again became engaged to a woman only to have her die very suddenly after a brief illness. Scriven was said to have then taken a radical Christian approach to life. He never refused to help anyone and shared all his possessions, even what little clothing he had for his own body. He devoted much time to helping the poor and handicapped, and did not charge for his services. He accidentally drowned in 1886.

Before Scriven's death a friend came to visit him when he was ill. The words to "What a Friend We Have in Jesus" were scribbled on a piece of paper next to the bed. The friend read the words and asked Scriven if he had written them. He humbly replied "The Lord and I did it between us."

Charles Converse wrote the tune for this hymn. He was a brilliant composer who studied in Germany and enjoyed the company of people such as Franz Liszt. He wrote two symphonies, several overtures, string quartets, oratorios, and hymn tunes. He is mainly remembered for composing the music for this hymn.

My simple fingerstyle arrangement is very basic and should be playable by most beginners. The advanced arrangement was done mostly by Ernie Smith. Ernie got the inspiration for this arrangement by listening to a version by pianist Roger Williams. Ernie worked on this arrangement for many years until he arrived at this final version. One unique aspect of this arrangement is the special tuning, which gives a very distinctive sound. Rick Foster suggested the faster-paced second half, and worked with Ernie to arrange this section. Rick first recorded this arrangement on his *Sacred Classic Guitar* album. I feel that this in one of the most beautiful and moving arrangements in this collection.

Melody-only version: Page 93

WHAT A FRIEND WE HAVE IN JESUS

Arranged for the
guitar by Gerard Garno

by Charles C. Converse

WHAT A FRIEND WE HAVE IN JESUS

Arranged for the guitar by
Ernie Smith and Rick Foster

Tune 6th To C
Tune 5th To G

by C.C. Converse

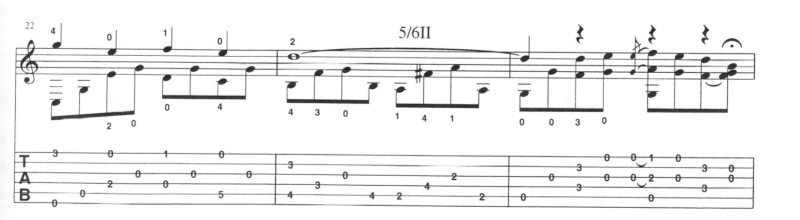

♩ = **104** Dotted eighth feel

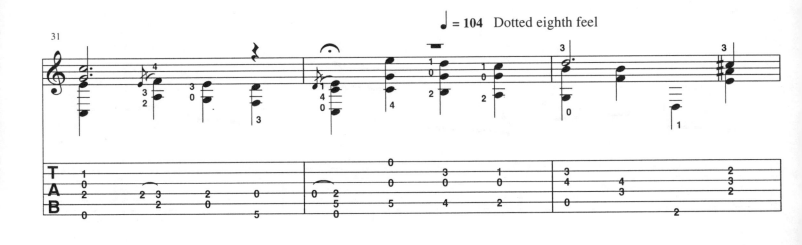

WHAT A FRIEND WE HAVE IN JESUS

Arranged for the guitar
by Gerard Garno

Words by Joseph M. Scriven
Music by Charles C. Converse

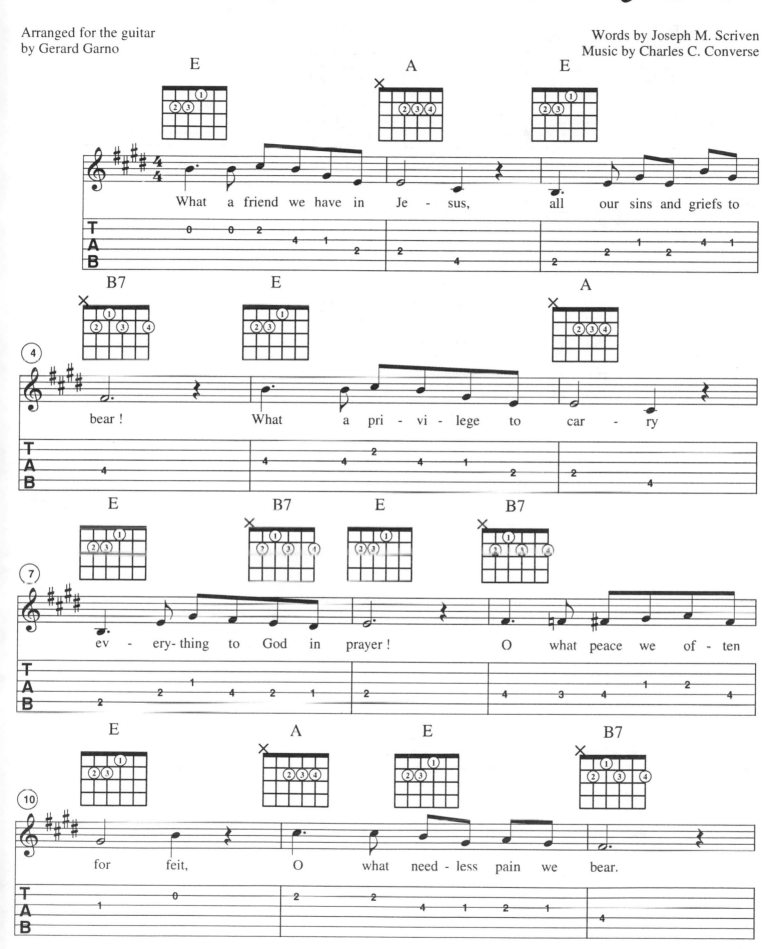

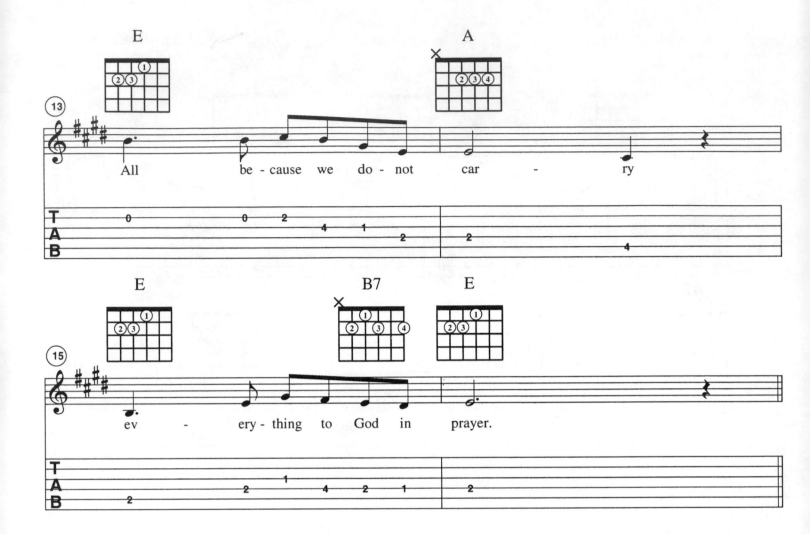

2. Have we trials and temptations? Is there trouble anywhere?
   We should never be discouraged; take it to the Lord in prayer.
   Can we find a friend so faithful, who will all our sorrows share?
   Jesus knows our every weakness; take it to the Lord in prayer.

3. Are we weak and heavy laden, cumbered with a load of care?
   Precious Savior still our refuge; take it to the Lord in prayer.
   Do thy friends despise, forsake thee? Take it to the Lord in prayer !
   In His arms He'll take and shield thee; thou wilt find a solace there.

I SURRENDER ALL

This hymn text was written by Judson W. Van de Venter. It was first published in the hymnal called *Gospel Songs of Grace and Glory* in 1896. Van de Venter was born on a farm near Dundee, Michigan, and later attended college in Hillsdale, Michigan. He went on to teach art in the public school. Following his successful involvement in evangelistic meetings at his church, he felt a call into full-time Christian work. He struggled with the decision for a time, and then decided to be an evangelist. Out of that struggle he found the inspiration to write this hymn text. The composer of the tune, W. S. Weeden, was an associate to Mr. Van de Venter.

My first fingerstyle arrangement is simple and yet it emphasizes the treble to bass voice response. The advanced arrangement is a virtuoso theme, with variations that I have revised and adapted from my first book called *Hymns and Sacred Melodies*, published by Mel Bay. While it was initially published as a straightforward classical style arrangement, I have spiced it up with plenty of "Tennessee twang!"

Melody-only version: Page 103

I SURRENDER ALL

Arranged for the guitar by
Gerard Garno

by W.S. Weeden

I SURRENDER ALL

Arranged for the guitar by
Gerard Garno

by W.S. Weeden

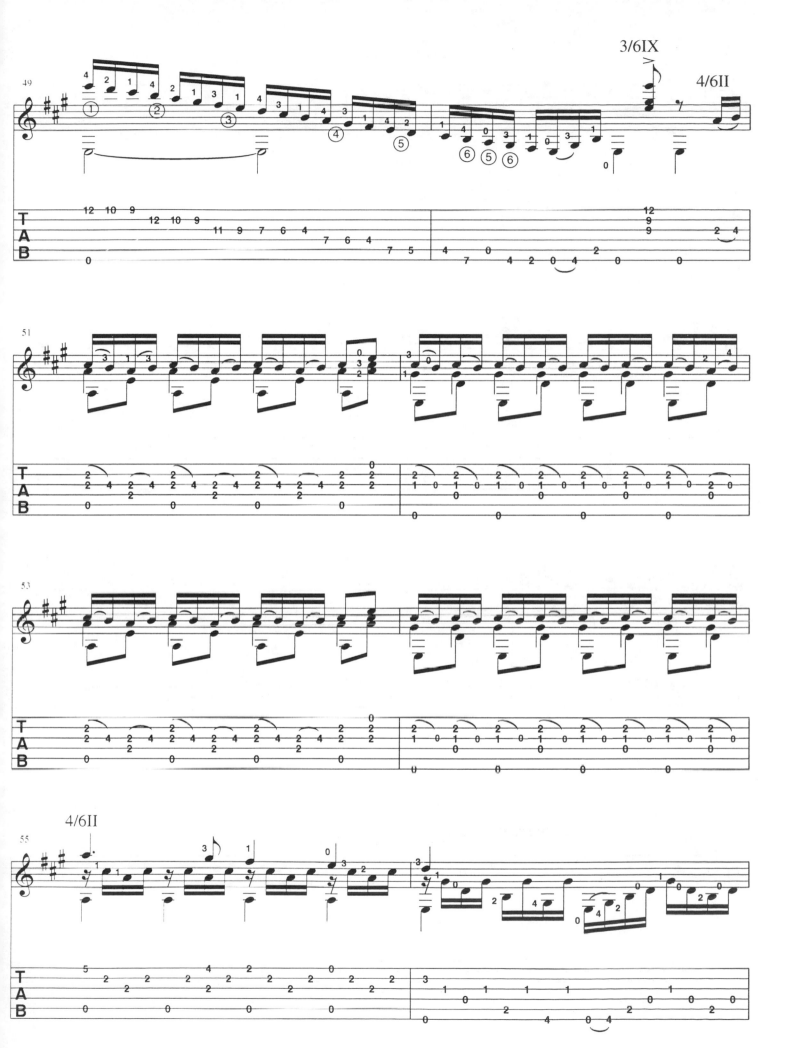

Return to the
beginning
and repeat theme

I SURRENDER ALL

Arranged for the guitar
by Gerard Garno

Words by J. W. Van Deventer
Music by W. S. Weeden

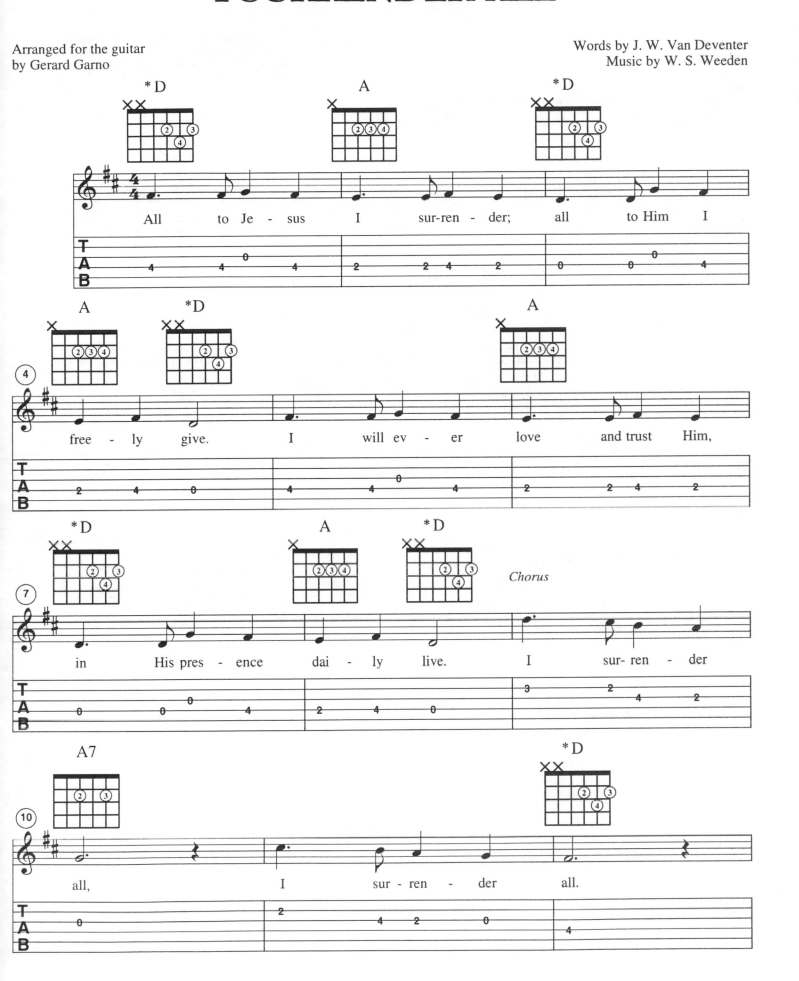

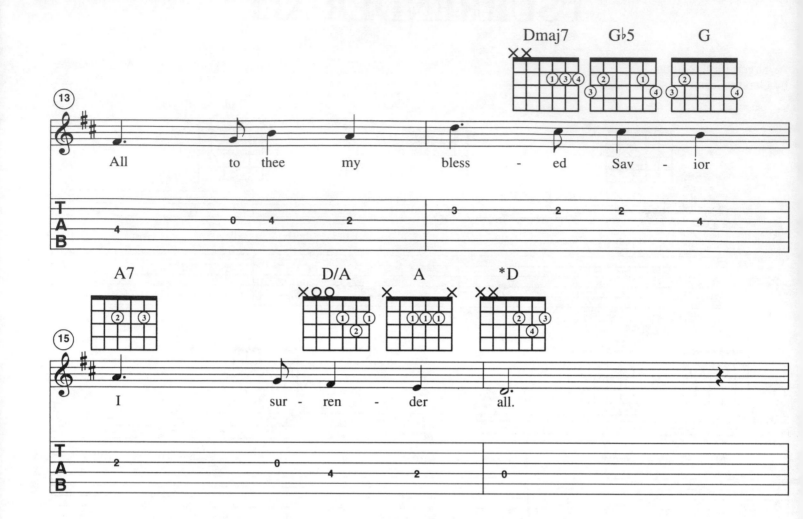

13 All to thee my bless - ed Sav - ior

Dmaj7   **G♭5**   **G**

A7   **D/A**   **A**   ***D**

15 I sur - ren - der all.

2. All to Jesus I surrender;
   Humbly at his feet I bow.
   Wordly pleasures all forsaken;
   Take me Jesus, take me now.
   Chorus

3. All to Jesus, I surrender;
   Make me, Savior, wholly thine.
   Let me feel the Holy Spirit,
   Truly know that thou art mine.
   ChorusA

4. All to Jesus I surrender;
   Lord, I give myself to thee.
   Fill me with thy love and power;
   Let thy blessing fall on me.
   Chorus

5. All to Jesus I surrender;
   Now I feel the sacred flame.
   O the joy of full salvation !
   Glory, glory to his name !
   Chorus

***D**

IN THE GARDEN

C. Austin Miles wrote this hymn text and tune in 1912 at the request of music publisher Dr. Adam Geibel. Miles gave the following account in George W. Sanville's book, *Forty Gospel Hymn Stories*:

"One day in March 1912, I was seated in the dark room where I kept my photographic equipment and organ. I drew my Bible toward me; it opened at my favorite chapter, John 20—whether by chance or inspiration let each reader decide. That meeting of Jesus and Mary had lost none of its power to charm. As I read it that day, I seemed to be a part of the scene. I became a silent witness to that dramatic moment in Mary's life, when she knelt before her Lord and cried, "Rabboni!"

My hands were resting on the Bible while I stared at the light blue wall. As the light faded, I seemed to be standing at the entrance to a garden, looking down a gently winding path, shaded by olive branches. A woman in white, with her head bowed, hand clasping her throat, as if to choke back her sobs, walked slowly into the shadows. It was Mary. As she came to the tomb, upon which she placed her hand, she bent over to look in, and hurried away.

John, in flowing robe, appeared, looked at the tomb; then came Peter, who entered the tomb, followed slowly by John. As they departed, Mary reappeared; leaning her head upon her arm at the tomb, she wept. Turning herself, she saw Jesus standing, so did I. I knew it was Jesus. Mary knelt before Him with arms outstretched and looking into His face and cried, "Rabboni!"

I awakened in full light, gripping the Bible, with tense muscles and nerves vibrating. Under the inspiration of this vision I wrote as quickly as the words could be formed, the poem exactly as it has since appeared. That same evening I wrote the music."

This is a very beautiful and emotional hymn, and I have made the arrangements to reflect that. Make sure not to play these solo arrangements too straight or cold.

I was inspired to arrange this hymn when I heard a duet version by Rick Foster on his *Sacred Classic Guitar* album. I did a shorter version for my book *Hymns and Sacred Melodies,* and have expanded this version to include key changes as well as a minor mode variation.

Melody-only version: Page 114

IN THE GARDEN

Arranged for the guitar
by Gerard Garno

by C. Austin Miles

IN THE GARDEN

Arranged for the guitar
by Gerard Garno

by C. Austin Miles

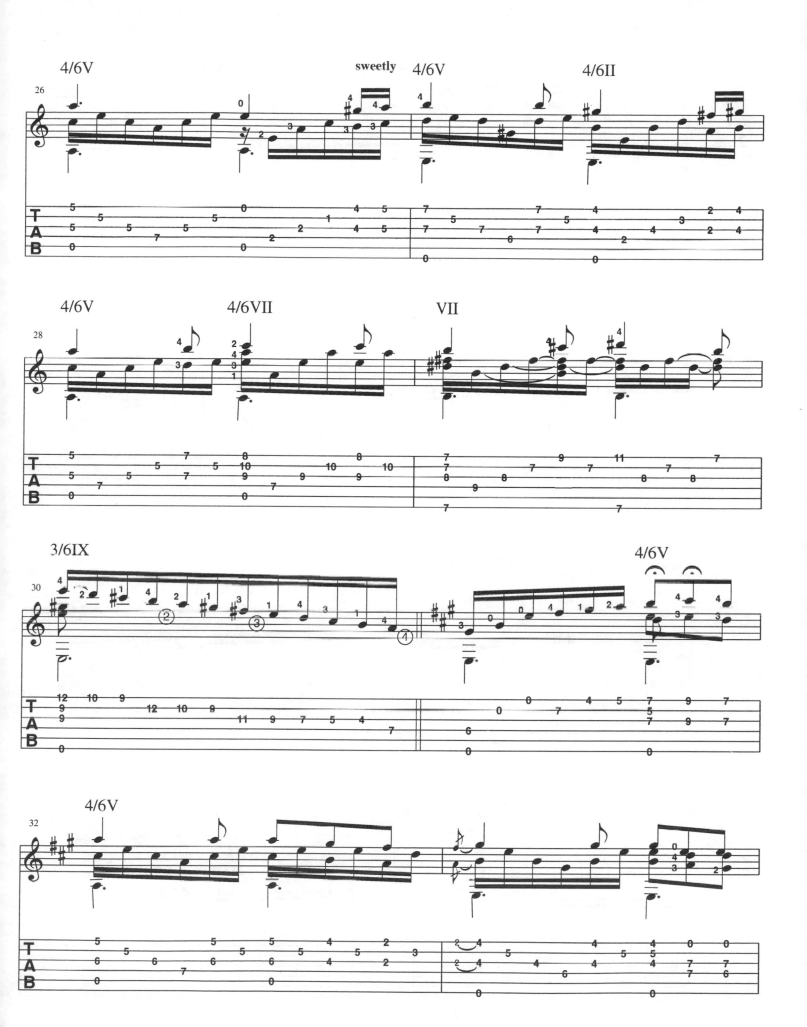

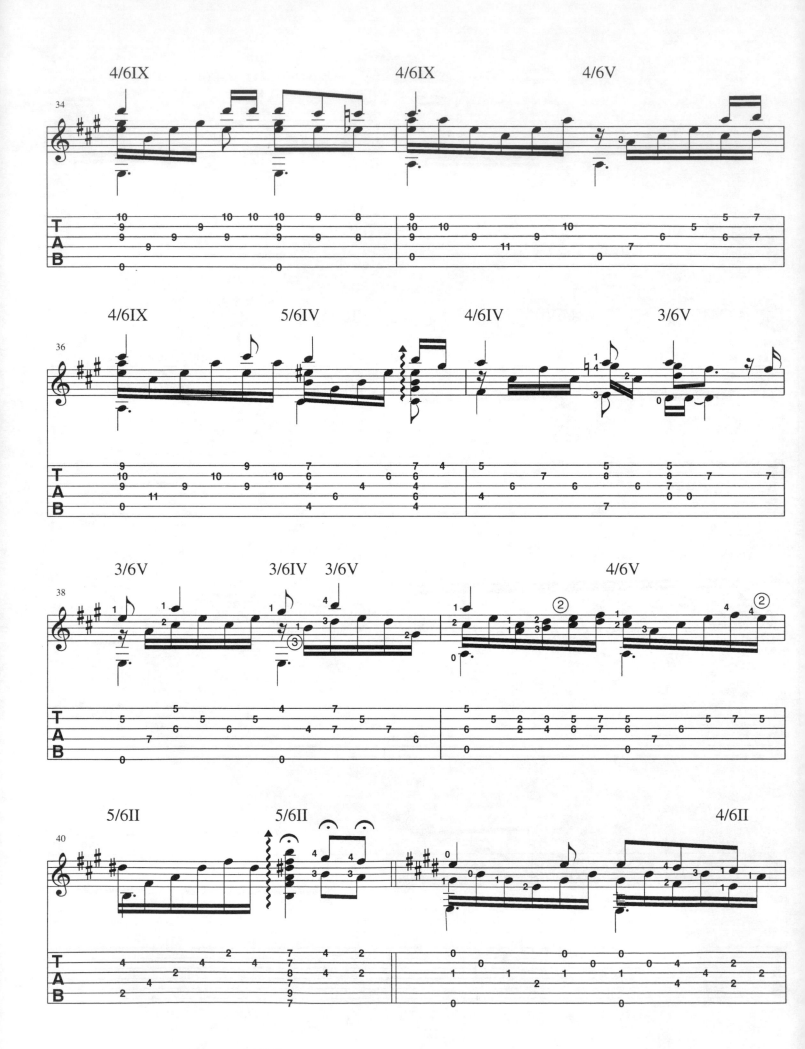

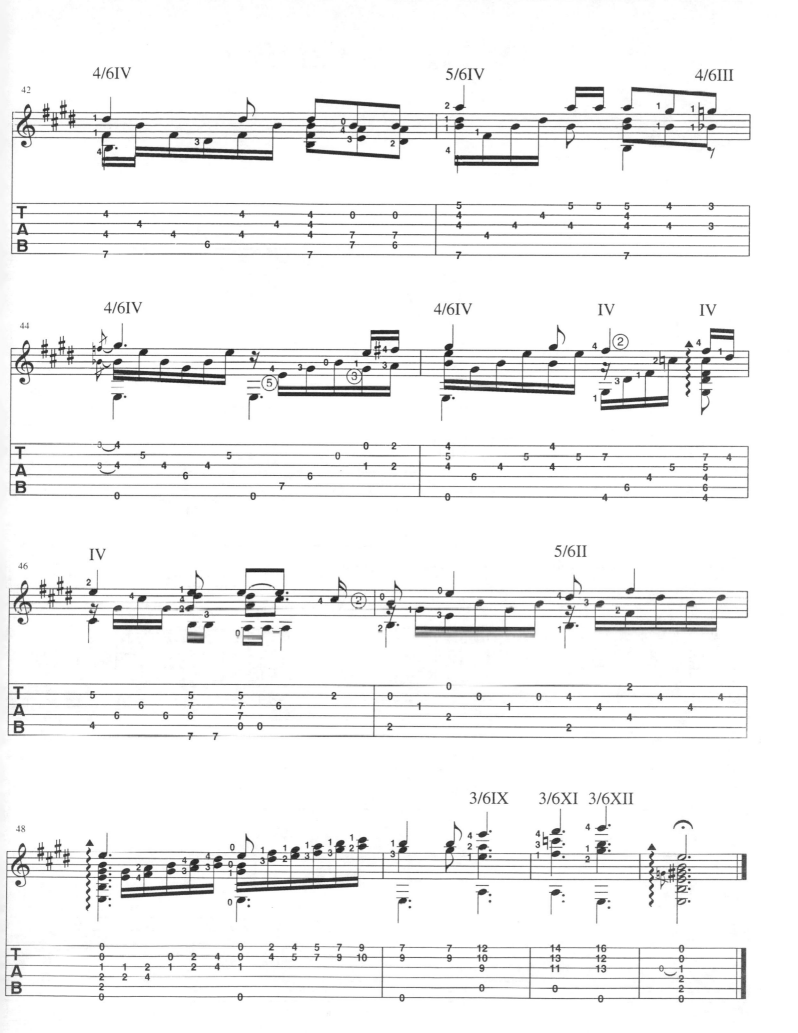

113

IN THE GARDEN

Arranged for the guitar
by Gerard Garno

Words and Music by
C. Austin Miles

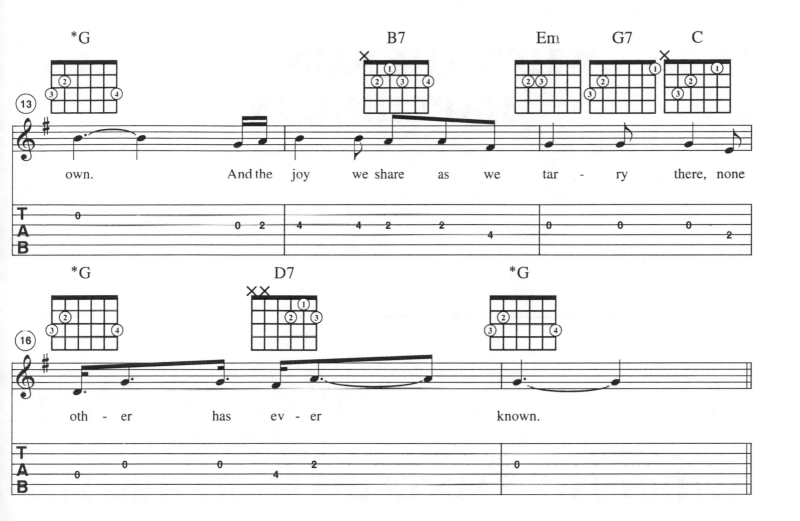

13 *G   B7   Em   G7   C

own.   And the   joy   we share   as   we   tar - ry   there, none

16 *G   D7   *G

oth - er   has   ev - er   known.

2. He speaks, and the sound of his voice, is so sweet the birds hush their singing.
   And the melody that he gave to me within my heart is ringing.
   Chorus

3. I'd stay in the garden with him, though the night around me falling.
   But he bids me go; thru the voice of woe his voice to me is calling.
   Chorus

*G

WHEN THE SAINTS GO MARCHING IN

Like "Swing Low Sweet Chariot," this is also a Negro spiritual that originated in America. A specific writer is not known. It is believed to have originated in the New Orleans area sometime around 1890, and was mainly used as a funeral march.

The first guitar arrangement I heard of this spiritual was by Ben Bolt in his album and book called *Holy Prelude*. I played Ben's arrangement for a while, and eventually did my own. My version uses key changes and some jazz flavor. The simple fingerstyle version is straightforward, using a melody line over an alternating bass pattern.

Melody-only version: Page 127

WHEN THE SAINTS GO MARCHING IN

Arranged for the guitar
by Gerard Garno

Traditional Afro-
American Spiritual

WHEN THE SAINTS GO MARCHING IN

Arranged for the guitar by
Gerard Garno

Traditional Afro-
American Melody

119

121

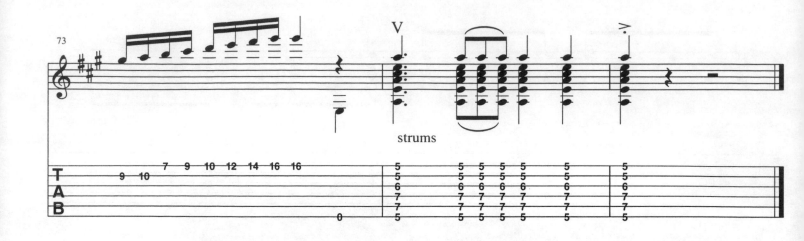

strums

WHEN THE SAINTS GO MARCHING IN

Arranged for the guitar
by Gerard Garno

Traditional American

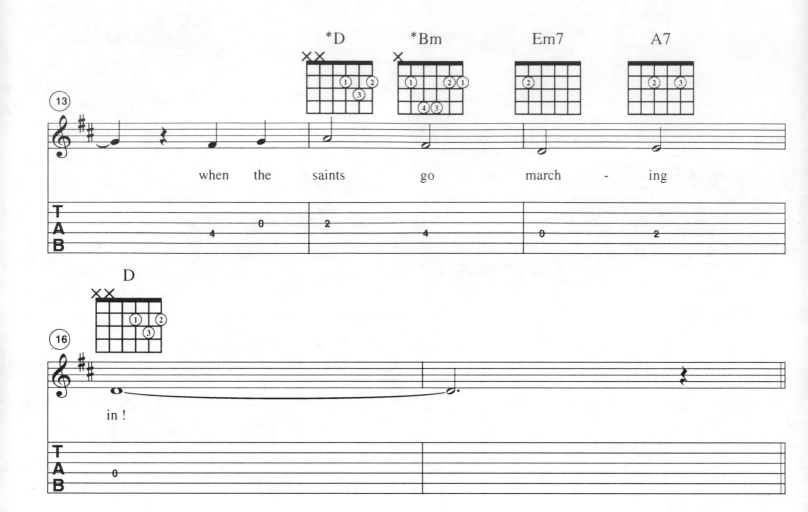

when   the   saints   go   march   -   ing

in !

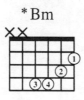

HOW GREAT THOU ART

In a 1974 *Christian Herald* magazine poll, this hymn was rated as the No. 1 hymn in America. The text for this hymn traces its roots back to a Swedish poem written by Rev. Carl Boberg in 1886, called "O Store Gud." He wrote the poem after experiencing a violent thunderstorm off the coast of Sweden, followed by some clear sunshine. He then noticed the singing of the birds and the beauty of creation, and he fell to his knees to worship God. He was inspired to write a nine-stanza poem. Churches in Sweden began to sing this poem to the tune of an old Swedish folk song. It was then translated into German and then a literal English translation was made by Rev. E. Gustav Johnson of North Park College, Chicago, Illinois, in 1925. In 1927 it was translated into Russian. Stuart Hine was a missionary working near Russia, and it was at that time that he became familiar with this hymn. Hine wrote his own verses based on the original poem.

The tune for this hymn is the traditional Swedish folk melody that has been arranged by Stuart K. Hine.

This hymn was introduced and made popular throughout America by the Billy Graham evangelistic team in the decade of the '50s.

My fingerstyle arrangements of this hymn were inspired and adapted from an arrangement by Chet Atkins and Rick Foster that appeared in Rick's book, *Inspirational Guitar at Its Best,* published by Mel Bay.

Melody-only version: Page 136

HOW GREAT THOU ART

Arranged for the guitar by
Gerard Garno

Traditional Swedish Melody

HOW GREAT THOU ART

Adapted and arranged for
the guitar by Gerard Garno

Traditional Swedish Melody

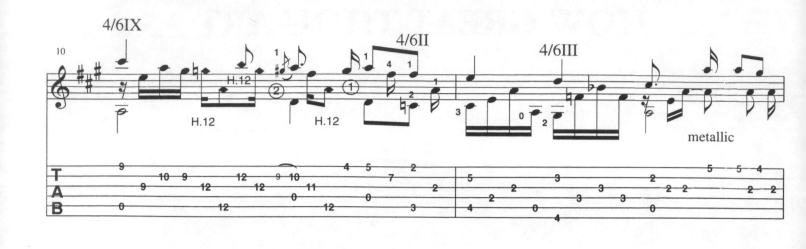

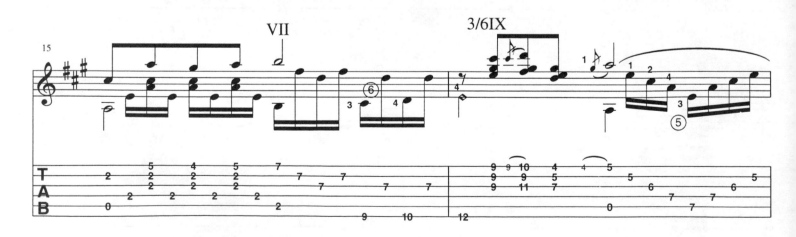

HOW GREAT THOU ART

Arranged for the guitar
by Gerard Garno

Words by Stuart K. Hine (translation)
Traditional Swedish Melody

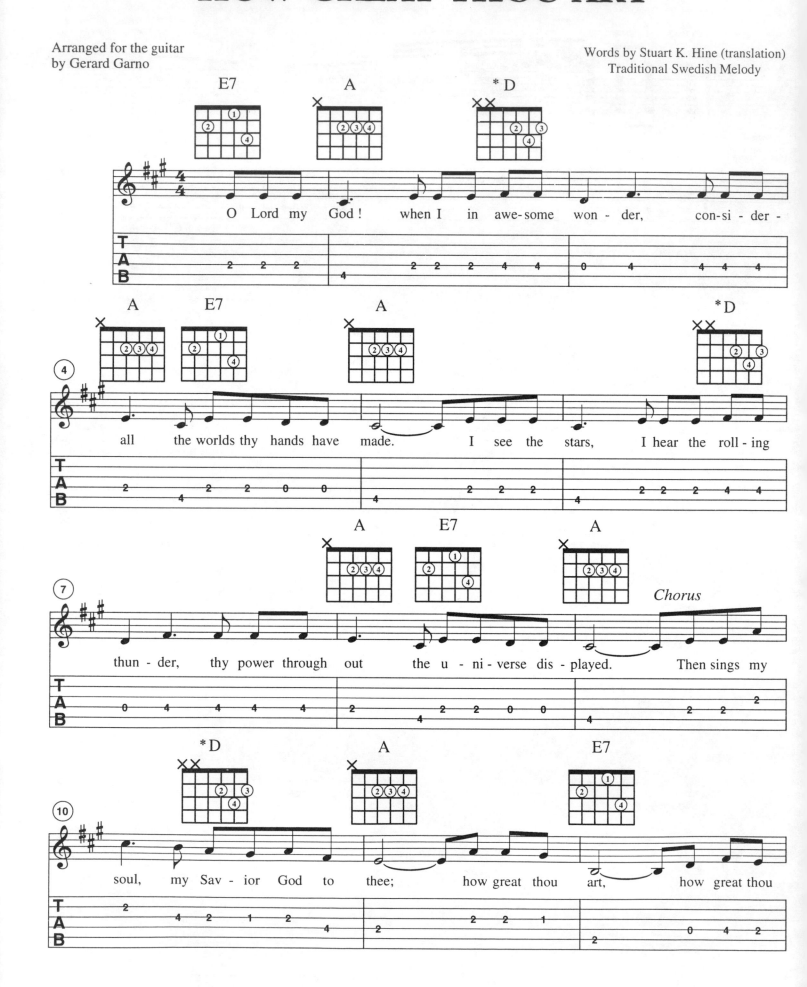

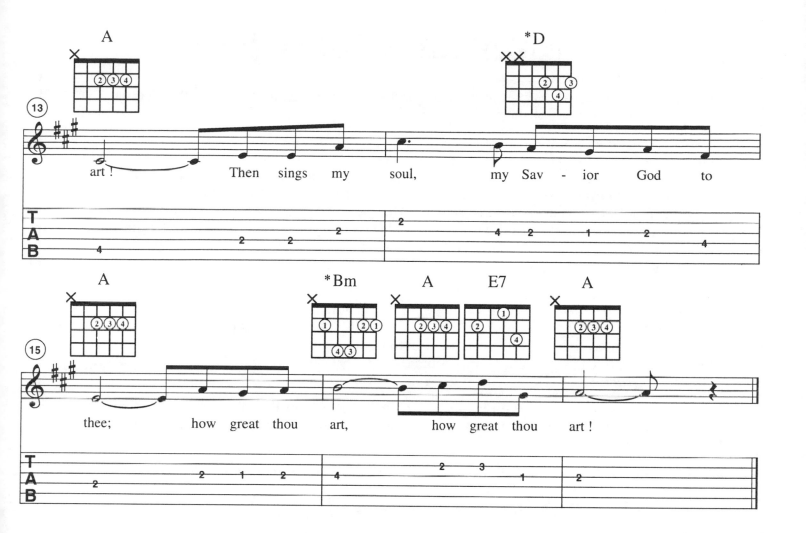

art ! Then sings my soul, my Sav - ior God to

thee; how great thou art, how great thou art !

2. When through the woods and forest glades I wander,
And hear the birds sing sweetly in the trees.
When I look down from lefty mountain granduer,
And hear the brook, and feel the gentle breeze.
Chorus

3. And when I think that God, his son not sparing,
Sent him to die, I scarce can take it in.
That on the cross, my burden gladly bearing,
He bled and died to take away my sin.
Chorus

4. When Christ shall come with shout of acclamation
And take me home, what joy shall fill my heart.
Then I shall bow, in humble adoration,
And there proclaim, my God how great thou art !
Chorus

AMAZING GRACE

English-born John Newton wrote the text for this hymn. It first appeared in the hymnal called *Olney Hymns*, published in 1779.

Newton quit school at the age of eleven to work with his father, who was a seaman. He led a very rebellious life, eventually getting involved in the slave trade. Later on, he bought his own slave ship and worked full-time at capturing, transporting and selling black slaves. During one very stormy voyage when it looked as if the ship may be lost, Newton first began to consider Christianity. After several more years as a slave trader, he became a Christian and started working to end slavery. He eventually became a minister in the Anglican Church. Sometime in the following years he wrote the famous text to "Amazing Grace."

The tune for this hymn is an early American folk melody. It was first published in a book called *The Virginia Harmony*, published in 1831 in Winchester, Virginia. Shortly thereafter this tune began to be combined with John Newton's text to create the version that is so well known today. Almost all subsequent hymn books have included this hymn. Its great impact on American culture was exemplified by a 1991 television special on P.B.S. called *Amazing Grace*.

My arrangements were inspired by a version that appeared in Rick Foster's book *Hymns for the Classic Guitar*. Rick adapted his arrangement from an earlier arrangement by Chet Atkins.

Melody-only version: Page 147

AMAZING GRACE

Arranged for the guitar by
Gerard Garno

Traditional American melody

AMAZING GRACE

Adapted and arranged for the
guitar by Gerard Garno

Traditional
American Melody

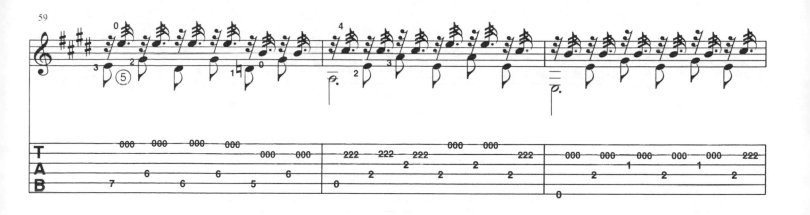

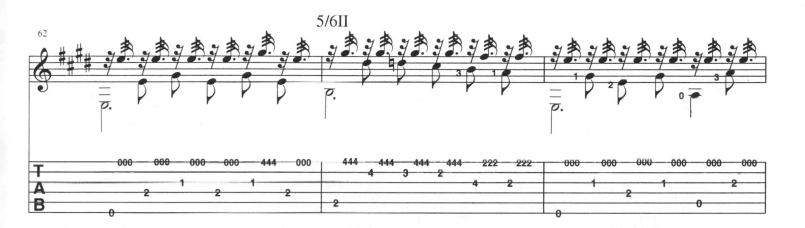

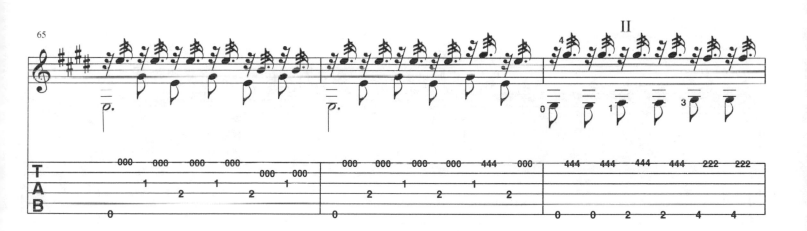

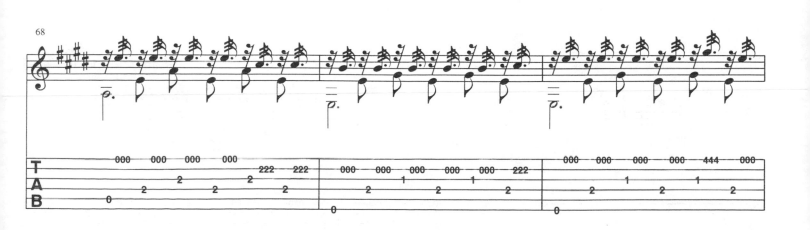

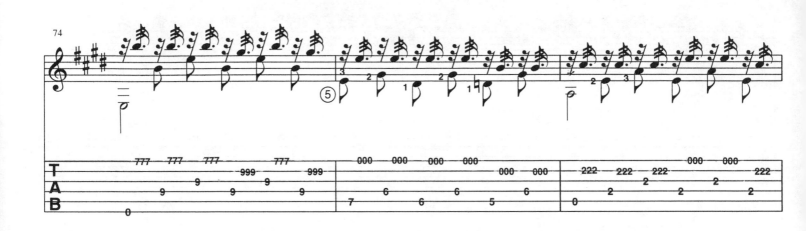

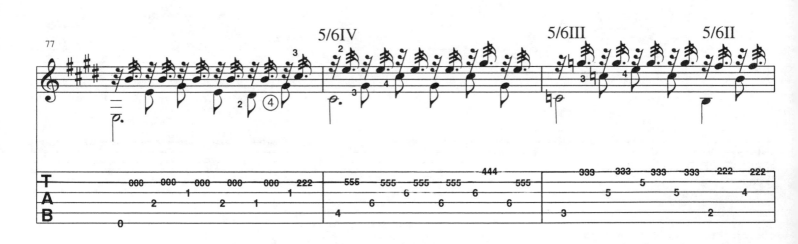

VAR. III
Same tempo as Var II

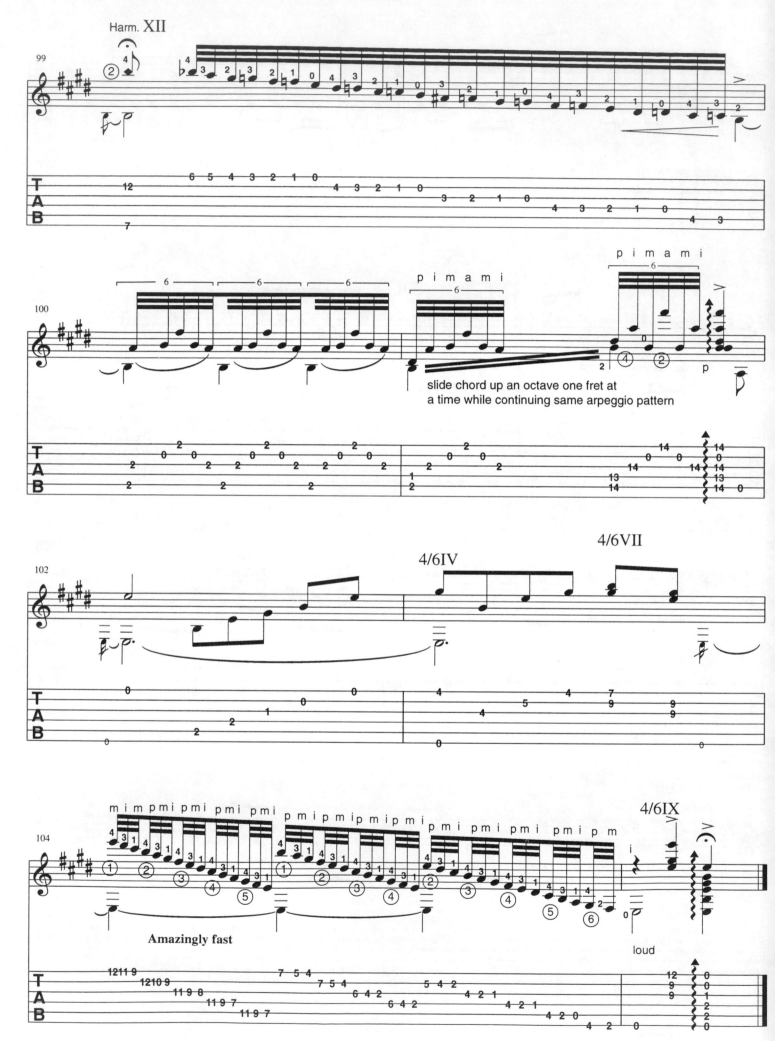

AMAZING GRACE

Arranged for the guitar
by Gerard Garno

Traditional American melody

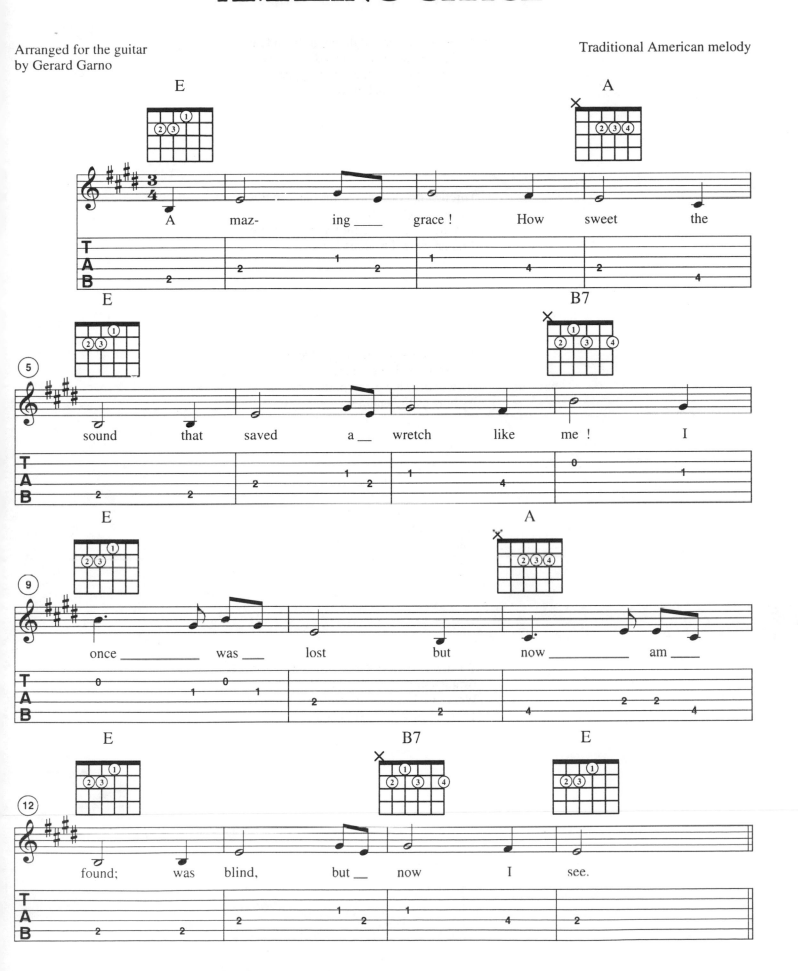

2. 'Twas grace that taught my heart to fear,
   And grace my fears relieved.
   How precious did that grace appear,
   The hour I first believed.

3. Through many dangers, toils and snares,
   I have already come.
   'Tis grace hath brought me safe thus far,
   And grace will lead me home.

4. The Lord has promised good to me,
   His word my hope secures.
   He will my shield and portion be,
   As long as life endures.

5. Yea, when this flesh and heart shall fail.
   And mortal life shall cease.
   I shall possess, within the veil,
   A life of joy and peace.

6. When we've been there ten thousand years,
   Bright shinning as the sun.
   We've no less days to sing God's praise,
   Than when we'd first begun.

THE UNCLOUDED DAY

This hymn was written by American pastor Josiah K. Alwood. John F. Kinsey harmonized it, and was the first to publish it in his book called *Living Gems* in 1890.

Like so many of these hymn writers, Josiah Alwood found his inspiration for this hymn in the biblical texts that talk about heaven and the promise of a better and even perfect life to come.

My simple fingerstyle arrangement is based on a alternating bass line. The advanced arrangement is by Rick Foster, and was first recorded by Rick on his album called *Sacred Classic Guitar*. It features a unique strumming and picking pattern that gives the impression of two guitars playing at one time.

In measure 8 of the simple fingerstyle arrangement a third-position bar is used. This may be a bit awkward. If it seems impossible to play this way, the first half of measure 8 may be fingered the same way as the first half of measure 10. A similar passage in measure 16 may be refingered as well.

Melody-only version: Page 160

THE UNCLOUDED DAY

Arranged for the guitar by
Gerard Garno

by J.K. Alwood

THE UNCLOUDED DAY

Arranged for the guitar by
Rick Foster

by J.K. Alwood

(strum 3 or 4 strings with index finger)

1/3I

(let bass notes ring throughout)
(brush down with index as thumb plays)

1/3I

155

(hold bass as long as possible)

1/3I

(pull off E to D)

1/3I

(unwritten B)

pull off from B in G7 chord

157

THE UNCLOUDED DAY

Arranged for the guitar
by Gerard Garno

Words and Music by
J.K.Alwood

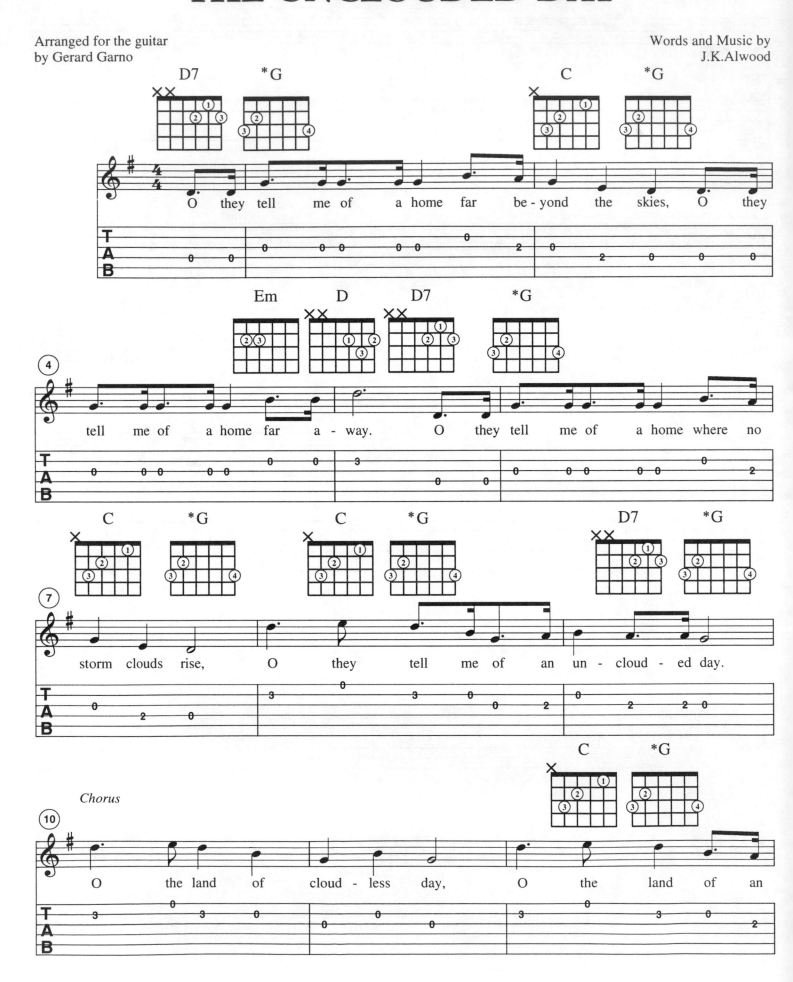

160

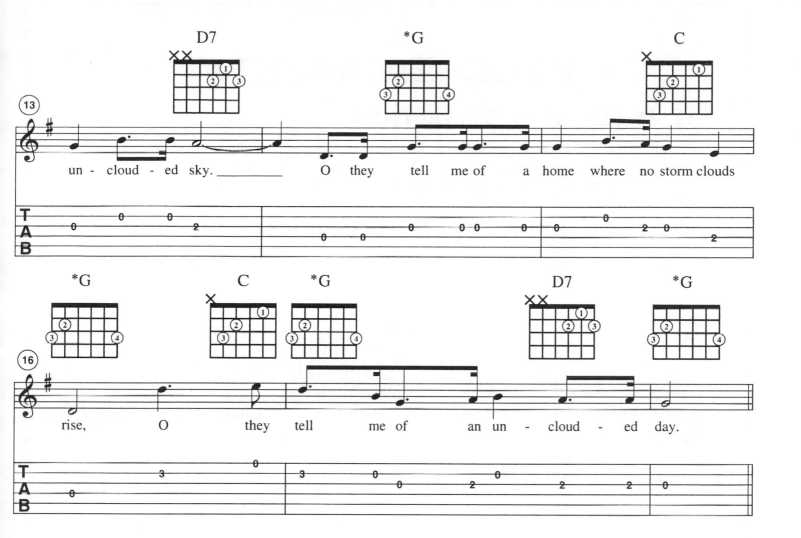

un - cloud - ed sky. _____ O they tell me of a home where no storm clouds rise, O they tell me of an un - cloud - ed day.

2. O they tell me of a home where my friends have gone,
O they tell me of that land far away.
Where the tree of life in eternal bloom,
Sheds its fragrance thru the unclouded day.
Chorus

3. O they tell me of the King in his beauty there,
And they tell me that mine eyes shall behold.
Where he sits on the throne that is whiter than snow,
In that city that is made of gold
Chorus

4. O they tell me that he smiles on his children there,
And his smiles drives their sorrows away.
And they tell me that no tears ever come again,
In that lovely land of unclouded day.
Chorus

PATRIOTIC MEDLEY

A) MY COUNTRY 'TIS OF THEE

Samuel Smith, a Baptist preacher from Boston, Massachusetts, wrote the text for this hymn. He graduated from Harvard in 1829. While meditating on the need for a good patriotic song for his young nation, he felt inspired to write the words to "My Country 'Tis of Thee." He wrote them on a piece of scrap paper in less than one-half of an hour.

The tune is a common one used for national anthems, including England's "God Save the King/Queen." It was first published in a hymnal called *Thesaurus Musicus* in 1740.

B) AMERICA THE BEAUTIFUL

Katherine Lee Bates wrote the text for this hymn in 1893. She got the inspiration while standing on Pike's Peak in Colorado, overlooking the beauty of God's creation. She also got inspiration from visiting Chicago that same year and viewing the spectacular buildings there. She believed that "We must match the greatness of our country with the goodness of personal Godly living."

The tune was composed by Samuel A. Ward years before the text was written. It was later joined with this hymn after many other tunes had been tried and proven unsatisfactory.

C) BATTLE HYMN OF THE REPUBLIC

This text was written by Julia Howe, and first published in 1862 in *The Atlantic Monthly* magazine. Mrs. Howe watched the troops go by day after day as they marched off to the Civil War singing "John Brown's Body," a song named after a self-styled abolitionist who was hanged after being caught trying to free slaves. Mrs. Howe's pastor suggested that she write some better words for the tune. She responded by writing the "Battle Hymn" that same evening.

The tune used for this hymn is a traditional Southern camp-meeting tune.

The advanced fingerstyle arrangement of this "Patriotic Medley" is by Tennessee guitarist Doyle Dykes. I first heard it on a recording that Doyle had made years ago, using an electric guitar and a band. It was immediately apparent that this arrangement was a masterpiece. I contacted Doyle and he graciously gave me permission to use it. Doyle is a great admirer of Chet Atkins, and Chet's influence on his style is very obvious.

The simple fingerstyle arrangements should present little difficulty. On measure 46 of the advanced arrangement, a fast and even rhythm section begins. In order to play this section smoothly and up to tempo, it is vitally important to observe the right-hand fingerings that I have included.

PATRIOTIC MEDLEY

Arranged for the guitar
by Doyle Dykes

1) My country 'tis of thee-from the thesarus musicas, 1744

♩ = 116 **sweetly with great feeling and rhythmic freedom**

♩ = 104   2) America the Beautiful - by Samuel Ward

5/6II

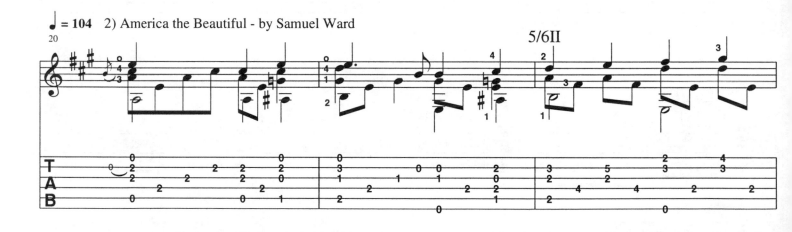

sweetly, pull the rhythm a bit

♩ = 84 loud and metallic 3) Battle hymn of the republic-19th cen. USA campmeeting tune

MY COUNTRY 'TIS OF THEE

Arranged for the guitar
by Gerard Garno

Traditional melody

MY COUNTRY 'TIS OF THEE

Arranged for the guitar
by Gerard Garno

Words by Samuel F. Smith
Traditional melody

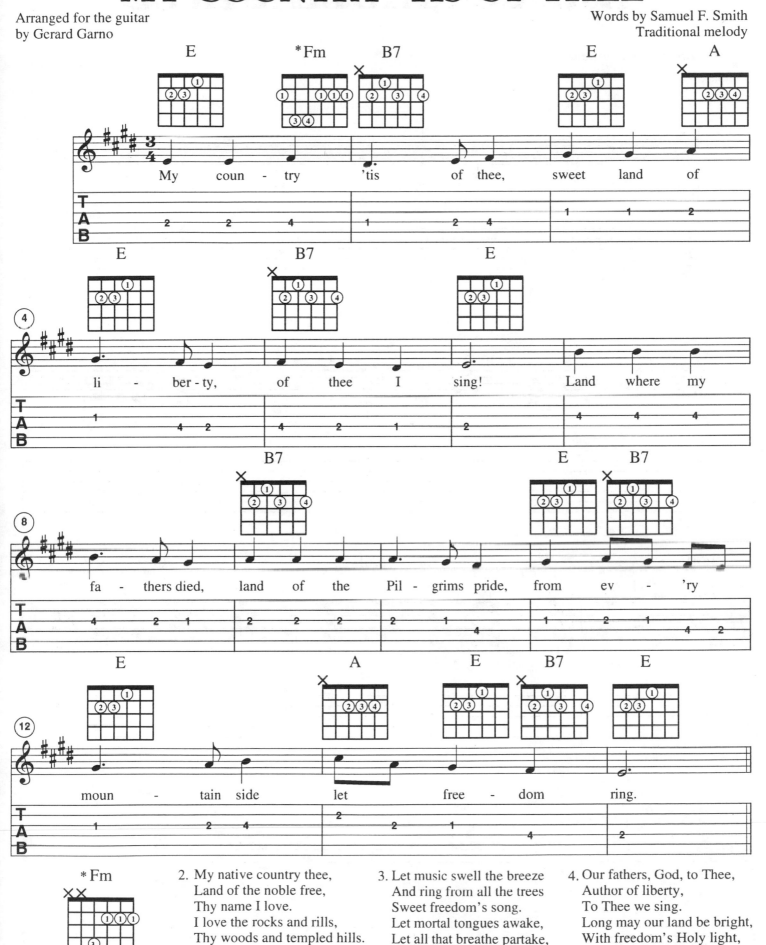

2. My native country thee,
Land of the noble free,
Thy name I love.
I love the rocks and rills,
Thy woods and templed hills.
My heart with rapture thrills,
Like that above.

3. Let music swell the breeze
And ring from all the trees
Sweet freedom's song.
Let mortal tongues awake,
Let all that breathe partake,
Let rocks their silence break,
The sound prolong.

4. Our fathers, God, to Thee,
Author of liberty,
To Thee we sing.
Long may our land be bright,
With freedom's Holy light,
Protect us by Thy might,
Great God, our King!

AMERICA THE BEAUTIFUL

Arranged for the guitar
by Gerard Garno

by Samuel A. Ward

AMERICA THE BEAUTIFUL

Arranged for the guitar
by Gerard Garno

Words by Katherine L. Bates
Music by Samuel A. Ward

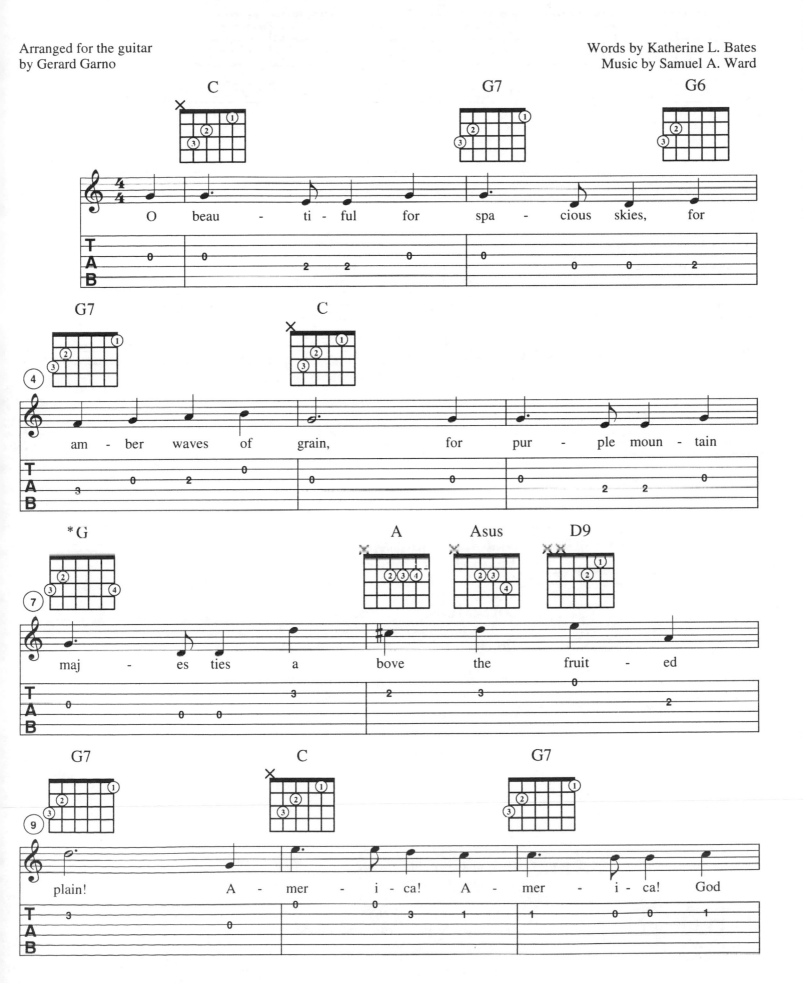

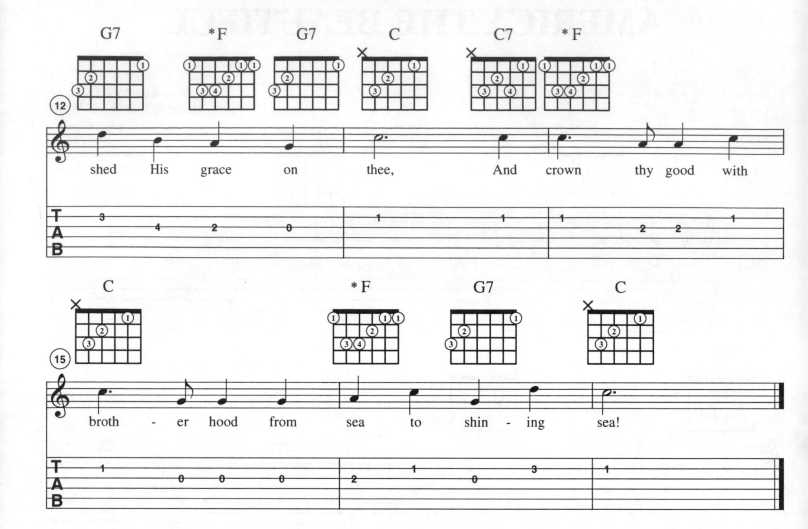

shed His grace on thee, And crown thy good with

broth - er hood from sea to shin - ing sea!

2. O beautiful for pilgrim feet,
   Whose stern, impassioned stress,
   A thoroughfare for freedom beat
   Across the wilderness!
   America! America!
   God mend thime every flaw,
   Confirm thy soul in self control,
   Thy liberty in law!

3. O beautiful for heros proved
   In liberating strife,
   Who more than self their country loved
   And mercy more than life!
   America! America!
   May God thy gold refine
   Till all success be nobleness
   And every gain divine!

4. O beautiful for patriot dream
   That sees beyond the years.
   Thine alabaster cities gleam,
   Undimmed by human tears!
   America! America!
   God shed His grace on thee,
   And crown thy good with brother hood
   From sea to shining sea!

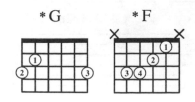

BATTLE HYMN OF THE REPUBLIC

Arranged for the guitar by
Gerard Garno

Traditional American melody

BATTLE HYMN OF THE REPUBLIC

Arranged for the guitar
by Gerard Garno

Words by Julia W. Howe
Traditional American melody

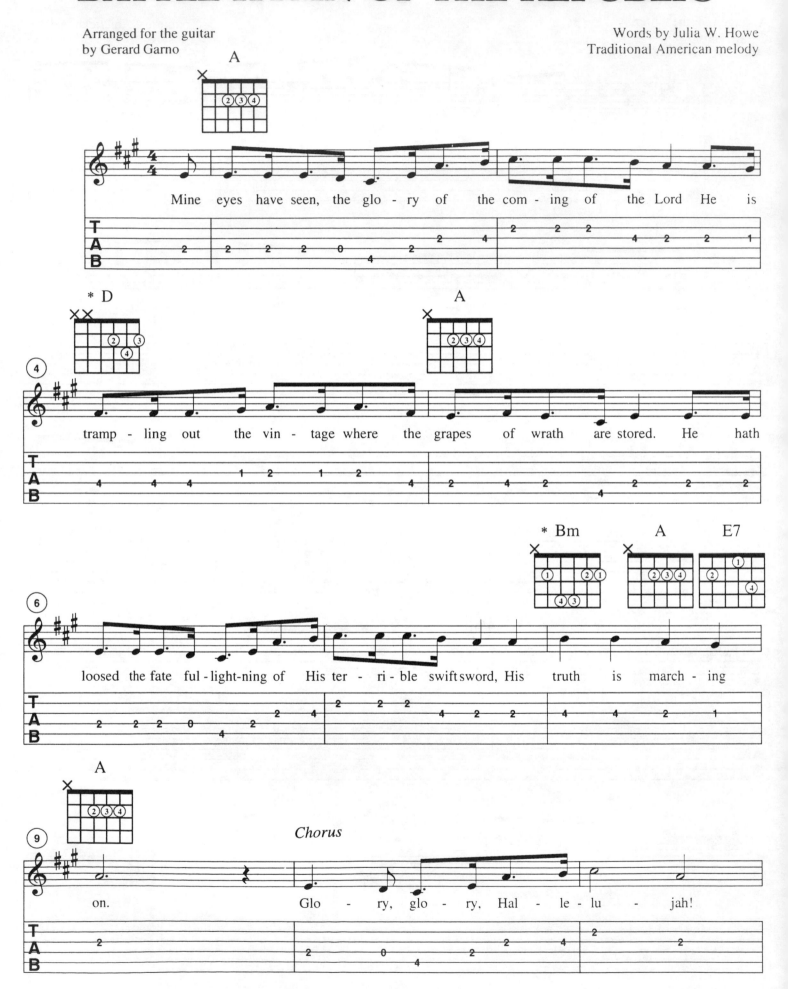

2. I have seen Him in the watchfires of a hundred circling camps;
   They have builded Him an alter in the evening dews and damps;
   I can read His righteous sentence by the dim and flaring lamps;
   His day is marching on.
   Chorus

3. He has sounded forth the trumpet that shall never sound retreat;
   He is sifting out the hearts of men before His judgement seat;
   O be swift my soul to answer Him, be jubilant, my feet!
   Our God is marching on.
   Chorus

4. In the beauty of the lilies Christ was born across the sea;
   With a glory in His bosom that transfigures you and me;
   As He died to make men holy, let us live to make men free,
   While God is marching on.
   Chorus

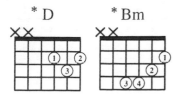

O HAPPY DAY

This hymn text was written by Phillip Doddridge, who is ranked along with Charles Wesley as one of England's finest eighteenth century hymn writers. It first appeared in 1755 in Job Orton's edition of Doddridge's writings, called *Hymns*.

The tune appeared about one hundred years after the text. It was adapted from a popular song by Edward F. Rimbault called "Happy Land." It first appeared in the book called *The Wesleyan Sacred Harp* by William McDonald in 1854.

An adaptation of this hymn was made by Edwin R. Hawkins in 1969. This version, re-corded by Hawkins, became a top-40 pop song. Most gospel artists use the contemporary Hawkins version.

My simple fingerstyle arrangement is arranged strictly from the old version. The advanced arrangement is based on an adaptation of both versions.

Melody-only version: Page 185

O HAPPY DAY

Arranged for the guitar by
Gerard Garno

by Edward F. Rimbault

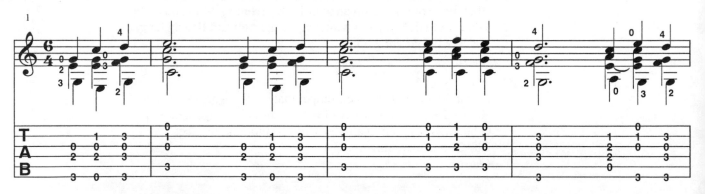

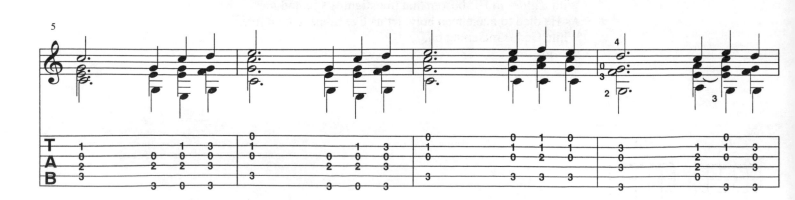

179

O HAPPY DAY

Arranged for the guitar
by Gerard Garno

By Edward F. Rimbault

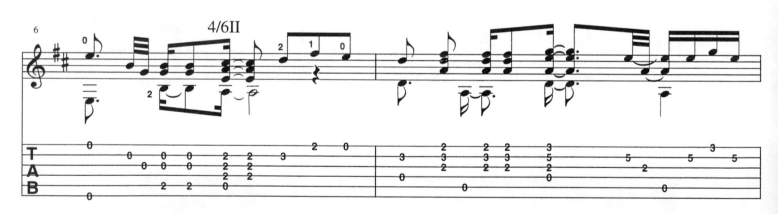

184

O HAPPY DAY

Arranged for the guitar
by Gerard Garno

Words by Philip Doddridge
Music by Edward F. Rimbault

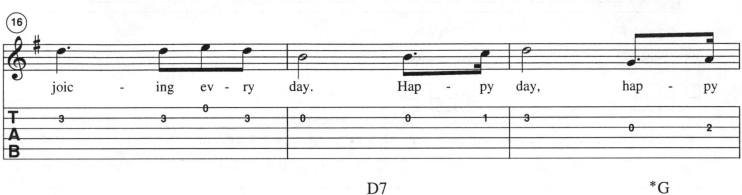

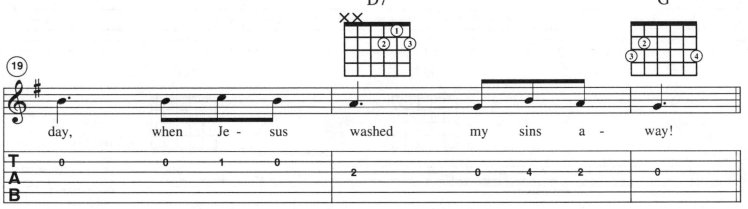

*G

2. O happy bond, that seals my vows,
   To him who merits all my love!
   Let cheerful anthems fill his house,
   While to that sacred shrine I move.
   Chorus

3. It's done the great transaction's done!
   I am the Lord's and he is mine.
   He drew me and I followed on,
   Charmed to confess the voice divine.
   Chorus

4. Now rest my long, divided heart,
   fixed on this blissful center, rest.
   Here have I found a nobler part;
   Here heavenly pleasures fill my breast.
   Chorus

5. High heaven that heard, the solemn vow,
   That vow renewed shall daily hear.
   Till in life's latest hour I bow,
   And bless in death a bond so dear.
   Chorus

BECAUSE HE LIVES

Bill and Gloria Gaither wrote this hymn in the late '60s. It was eventually voted song of the year in 1974 by the Gospel Music Association and ASCAP.

The Gaithers say that the inspiration for this song was the birth of their third child, Benji. During the time they were expecting him, America was going through the Vietnam War, the drug-culture explosion, the sexual revolution, etc. The Gaithers had to wonder what kind of a world they were bringing their child into, but they were reassured that because He lives, life was still worth living and facing tomorrow. It was out of these circumstances that "Because He Lives" was born as a song of encouragement to themselves and others.

Having met the Gaithers and been encouraged by them, I was all the more excited to arrange this favorite song that they wrote. I have kept both of the fingerstyle arrangements fairly simple in a effort not to obscure the simple beauty of this hymn.

Melody-only version: Page 192

BECAUSE HE LIVES

Arranged for the guitar
by Gerard Garno

by William J. Gaither

188

BECAUSE HE LIVES

Arranged for the guitar
by Gerard Garno

by William J. Gaither

191

BECAUSE HE LIVES

Arranged for the guitar
by Gerard Garno

Words by Gloria and William J. Gaither
Music by William J. Gaither

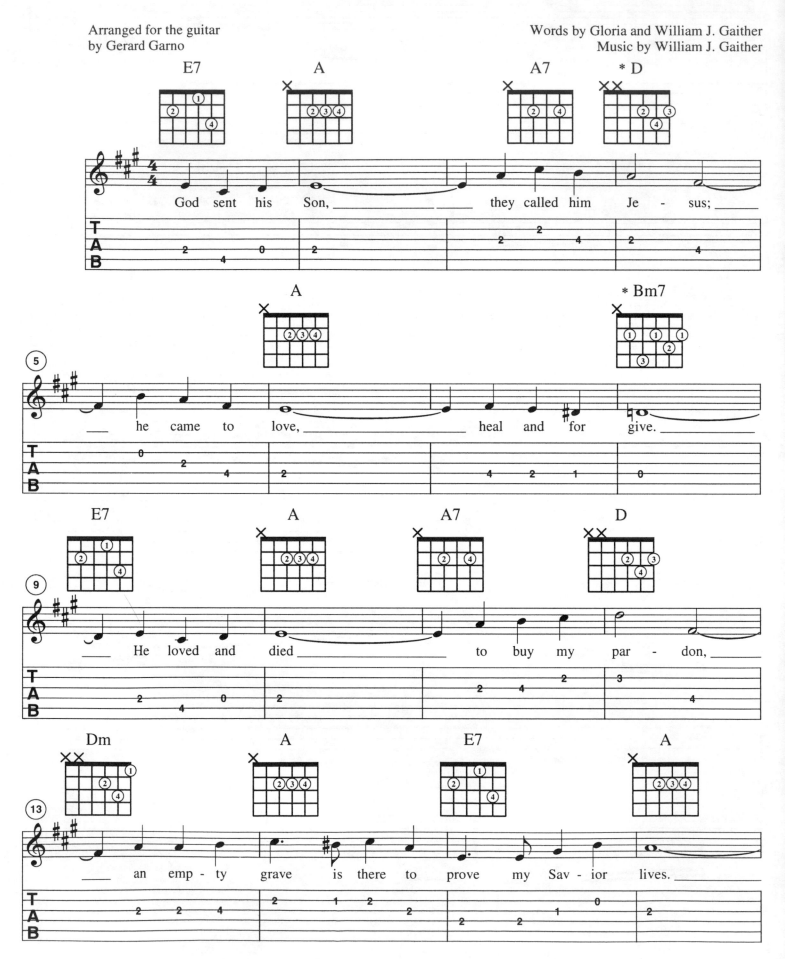

2. How sweet to hold a new born baby,
   And feel the pride and joy he gives.
   But greater still the calm assurance,
   This child can face uncertain days because he lives.
   Chorus

3. And then one day I'll cross the river;
   I'll fight life's final war with pain.
   And then as death gives way to victory
   I'll see the lights of glory and I'll know he reigns.
   Chorus

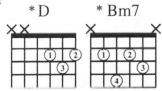

THERE IS POWER IN THE BLOOD

While attending a camp meeting at Mountain Lake Park, Maryland, Lewis E. Jones was inspired to write the words and music for this great hymn. The manuscript was then sold to Dr. H. L. Gilmour, who was the first to publish it in a hymnal called *Songs of Praise and Victory*, in 1899.

I have arranged the simple fingerstyle arrangement over an alternating country bass pattern. The advanced arrangement was masterfully arranged by Ernie Smith. Ernie says that he first played this hymn while he was performing in an Assembly of God church orchestra as a child. He liked the song because of the story of salvation it tells. He arranged it in a rhythmic, up-tempo style.

Melody-only version: Page 202

THERE IS POWER IN THE BLOOD

Arranged for the guitar by
Gerard Garno

words and music by L.E. Jones

194

THERE IS POWER IN THE BLOOD

Arranged for the
guitar by Ernie Smith

by L.E. Jones

sweetly

loud

loud and sweet

3/6II

loud and metallic

sweetly

getting, louder

metallic   growing slower

back to an even rhythm

repeat last section several times
while adding runs and fading out

201

THERE IS POWER IN THE BLOOD

Arranged for the guitar
by Gerard Garno

Words and Music by
L.E.Jones

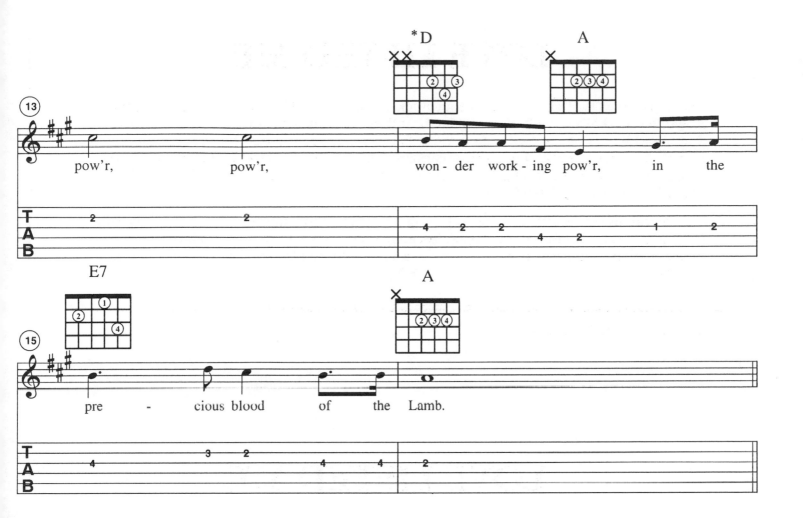

pow'r, pow'r, won - der work - ing pow'r, in the
pre - cious blood of the Lamb.

*D

2. Would you be free from your passion and pride?
   There's pow'r in the blood, pow'r in the blood.
   Come for a cleansing to Calvary's tide.
   There's wonderful pow'r in the blood.;
   Chorus

3. Would you be whiter, much whiter than snow?
   There's pow'r in the blood, pow'r in the blood.
   Sin stains are lost in its life giving flow;
   There's wonderful pow'r in the blood.
   Chorus

4. Would you do service for Jesus your King?
   There's pow'r in the blood, pow'r in the blood.
   Would you live daily his praises to sing?
   There's wonderful pow'r in the blood.
   Chorus

LOVE LIFTED ME

This hymn was written in 1912 in Saugatuck, Connecticut. The writer of the text, James Rowe, worked along with Howard Smith as they wrote this hymn. It is said that Howard Smith had hands so knotted with arthritis that it was a miracle that he could even play the piano. On June 1, 1912, the hymn was purchased and copyrighted by Charlie D. Tillman. It was then sold to Robert H. Coleman on May 25, 1915. Coleman first published the song in his hymnal called *The Herald*.

This hymn always impressed me as having a very attractive melody. I remember hearing it sung in a Baptist church and being inspired to arrange it for guitar. Both of my fingerstyle arrangements are fairly simple, and should be playable by guitarists of moderate ability.

Melody-only version: Page 211

LOVE LIFTED ME

Arranged for the guitar
by Gerard Garno

by Howard E. Smith

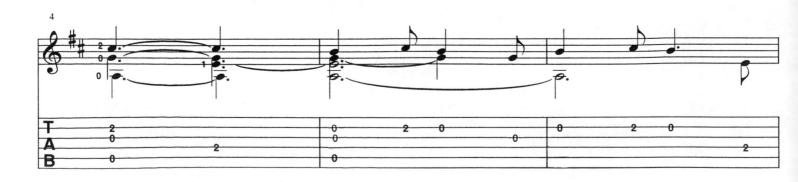

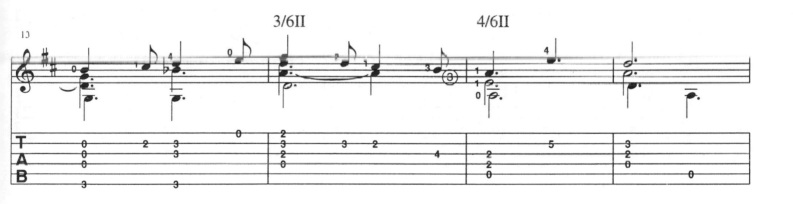

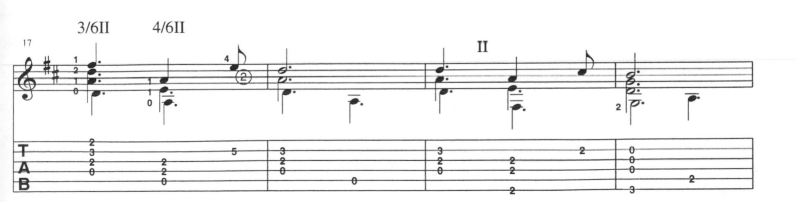

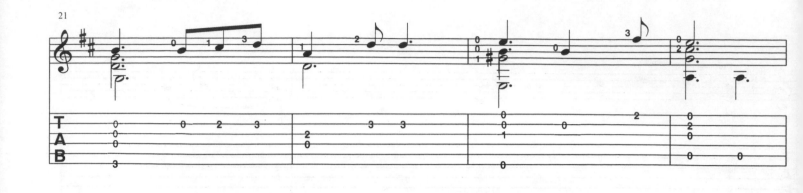

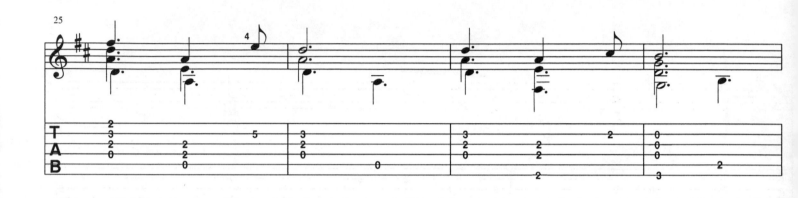

LOVE LIFTED ME

Arranged for the guitar
by Gerard Garno

by James Rowe

208

LOVE LIFTED ME

Arranged for the guitar
by Gerard Garno

Words by James Rowe
Music by Howard E. Smith

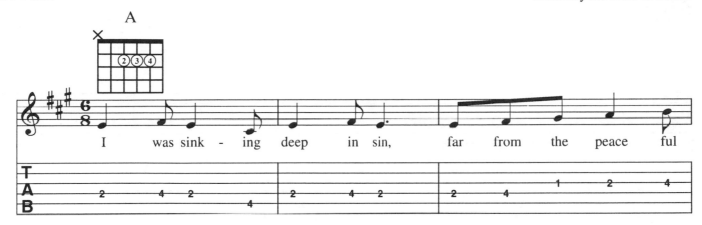

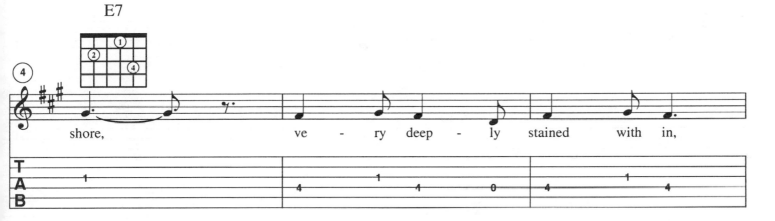

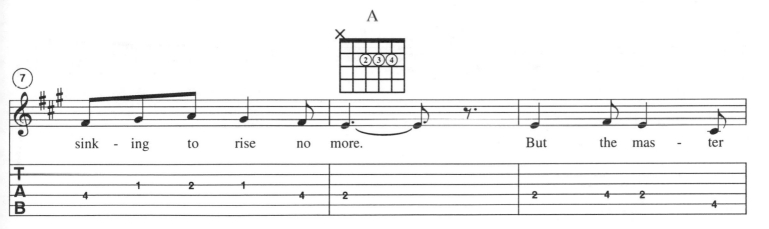

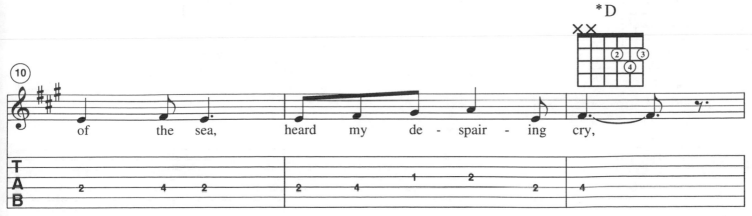

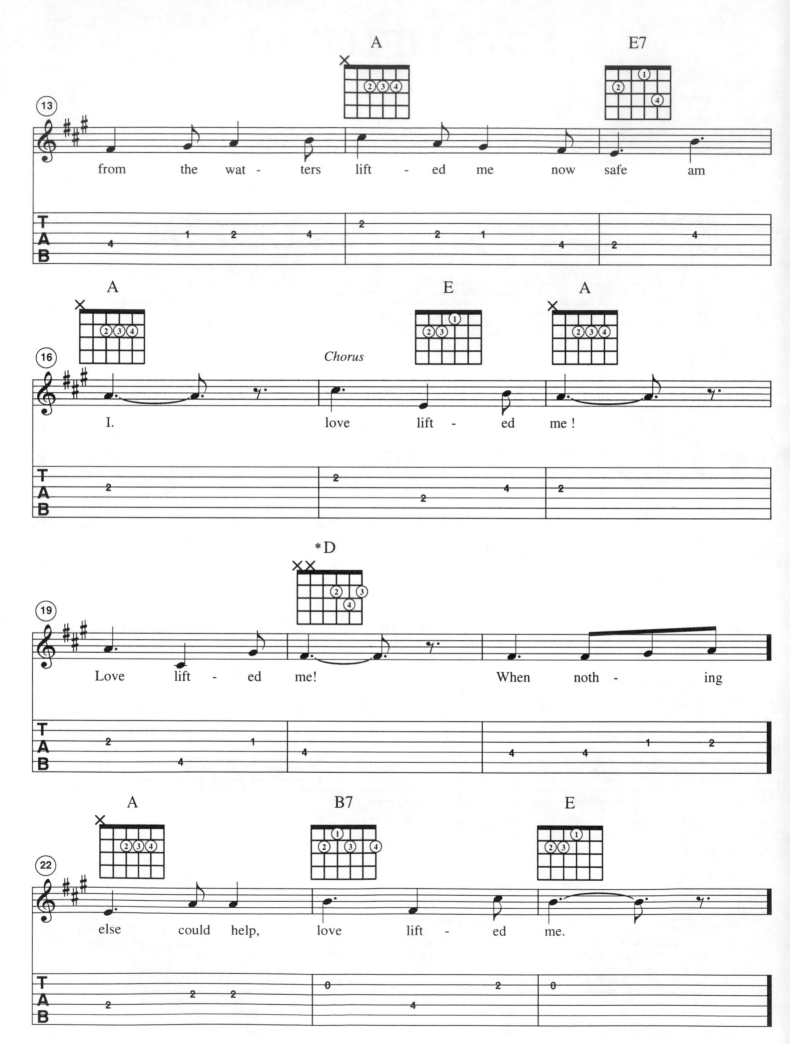

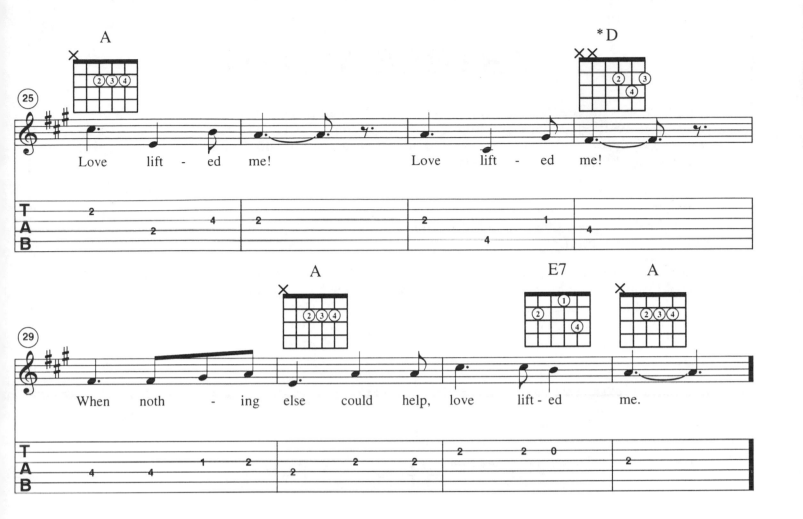

Love lift - ed me! Love lift - ed me!

When noth - ing else could help, love lift - ed me.

2. All my heart to him I give, ever to him I'll cling,
   In his blessed presence live, ever his praises sing.
   Love so mighty and so true, merits my soul's best songs,
   Faithful, loving service, too, to him belongs.
   Chorus

3. Souls in danger, look above, Jesus completely saves,
   He will lift you by his love out of the angry waves.
   He's the Master of the sea, billows his will obey,
   He your Savior wants to be —be saved today.
   Chorus

*D

213

FARTHER ALONG

The first appearance of this hymn was in a book called *Select Hymns for Christian Worship*, arranged, edited, and published by B. E. Warren in 1911. It appeared in this book as text only, with no tune. In 1937, the text and tune were published in a book called *Starlit Crown*, published by the Stamps-Baxter Music Company.

W. B. Stevens says that he wrote this song as he wondered why Christians, including himself, seemed to suffer so much while other people seemed to prosper. He could only look forward to the time when we would enter our heavenly home and all our questions would be answered.

With the possible exception of some of the second-position bars, my simple arrangement should present few technical difficulties. The advanced arrangement is by Ernie Smith. Ernie said that he grew up hearing this song in church. However, he did not attempt to arrange it for solo guitar until he heard an arrangement by Chet Atkins on a 1962 album from RCA. Chet's arrangement inspired Ernie to do the arrangement that I have included here.

Melody-only version: Page 223

FARTHER ALONG

Arranged for the guitar by
Gerard Garno

by W. B. Stevens

FARTHER ALONG

Arranged for the
guitar by Ernie Smith

by W.B. Stevens

218

219

222

FARTHER ALONG

Words and Music by
W.B. Stevens

Arranged for the guitar
by Gerard Garno

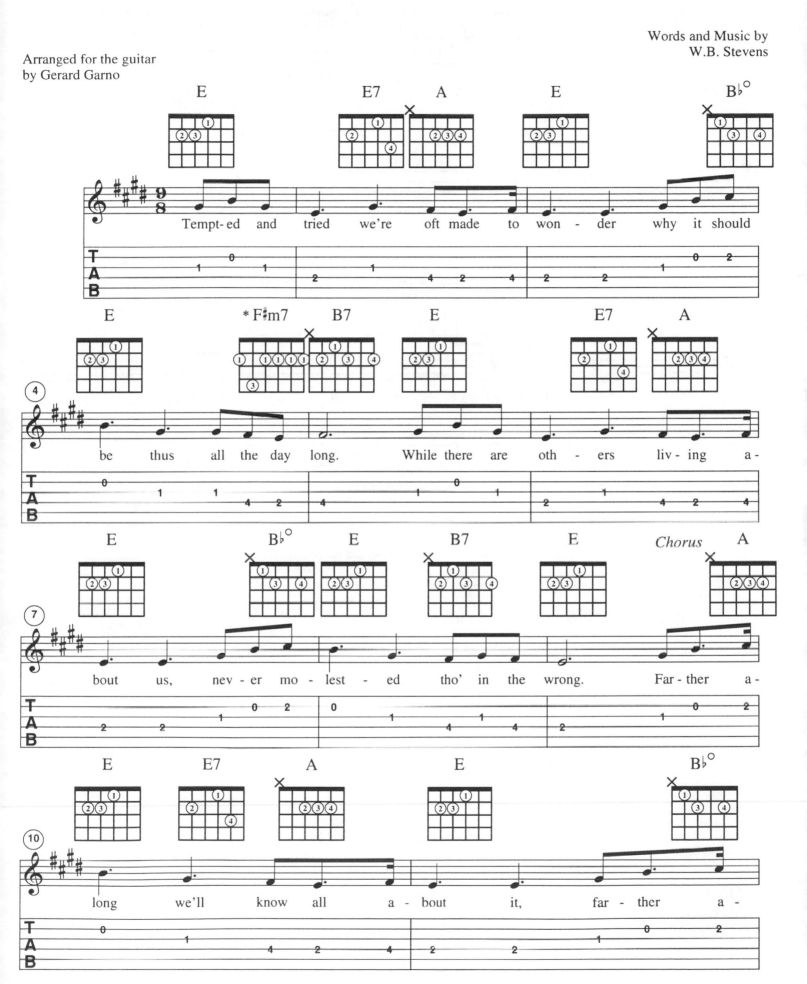

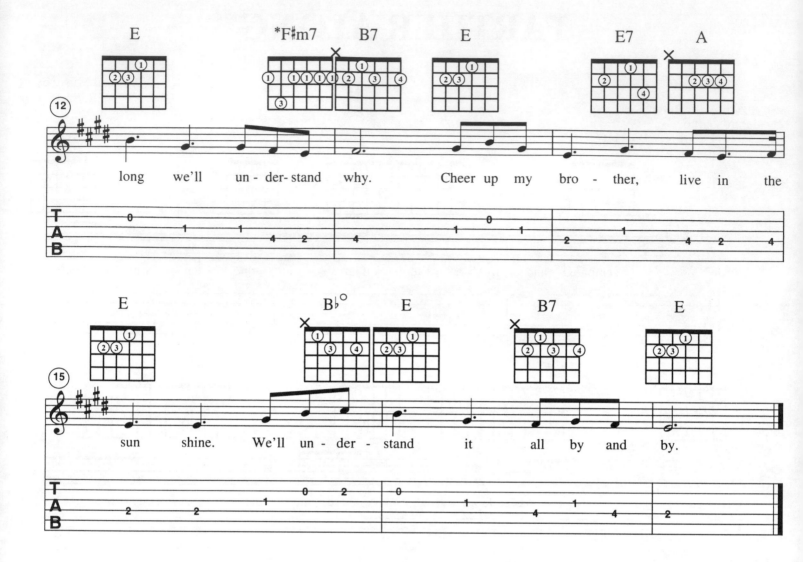

long we'll un-der-stand why. Cheer up my bro - ther, live in the

sun shine. We'll un - der - stand it all by and by.

2. When death has come and taken our loved ones,
   It leaves our home so lonely and drear.
   Then do we wonder why others prosper,
   Living so wicked year after year.
   Chorus

3. "Faithful to death" said our loving Master,
   A few more days to labor and wait.
   Toils of the road will then seem as nothing,
   As we sweep thru the beautiful gate.
   Chorus

4. When we see Jesus coming in glory,
   When he comes from his home in the sky.
   Then we shall meet him in that bright mansion,
   We'll understand it all by and by.
   Chorus

*F♯m7

BLESSED ASSURANCE

Fanny Crosby is estimated to have written more than 8,000 gospel song texts during her lifetime. This is a truly amazing achievement, especially considering that she was blind. Many times the themes for her hymns were suggested by ministers wanting a song on a particular subject. Or, a person presented her with a tune and asked her to compose the text. This latter method was the one used to birth "Blessed Assurance." An amateur musician named Mrs. Joseph Knapp, a friend of Fanny's, wrote a tune and played it for her. She asked Fanny what she thought the tune said. To this, Fanny responded "Why, that says: Blessed Assurance, Jesus is Mine!" Fanny then proceeded to write the entire text. This hymn was first published in 1873 in a book called *Gems of Praise*, by J. R. Sweeny. It was then included in Sankey's *Sacred Songs and Solos* in England, and the *Gospel Hymn* series in America. This hymn became extremely popular on both sides of the Atlantic.

My simple fingerstyle arrangement should present few difficulties. However, in measure 9, there is a third-position barring section that may seem a bit awkward at first. The advanced arrangement is based on a unique rhythmic pattern with a free and lyrical middle section.

Melody-only version: Page 234

BLESSED ASSURANCE

Arranged for the guitar
by Gerard Garno

by Phoebe P. Knapp

BLESSED ASSURANCE

Arranged for the guitar
by Gerard Garno

by Phoebe P. Knapp

228

2nd time to ⊕

BLESSED ASSURANCE

Arranged for the guitar by
Gerard Garno

Words by Fanny J. Crosby
Music by Phoebe P. Knapp

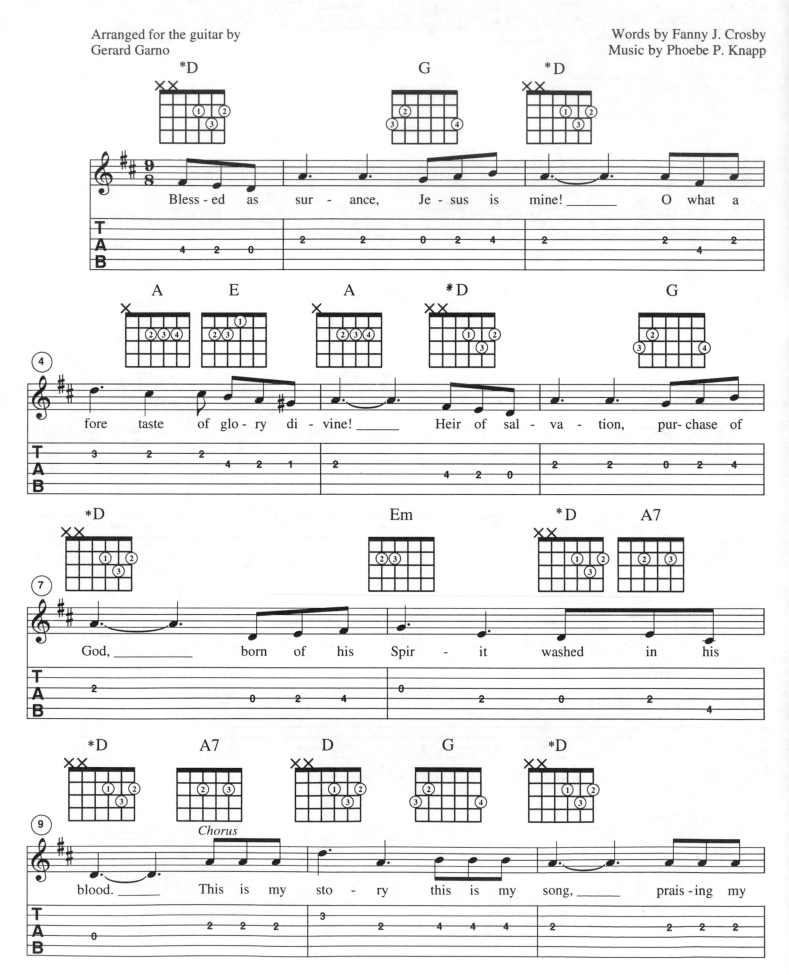

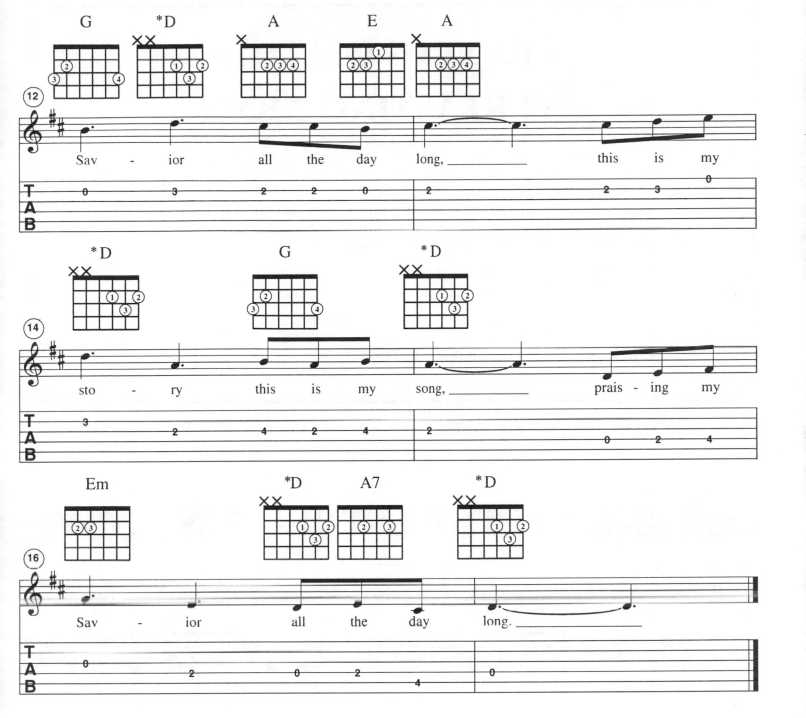

2. Perfect submission, perfect delight,
   Visions of rapture now burst on my sight.
   Angels decending bring from above,
   Echoes of mercy, whispers of love.
   Chorus

3. Perfect submission, all is at rest,
   I in my Savior am happy and blest.
   Watching and waiting, looking above,
   Filled with his goodness, lost in his love.
   Chorus

*D

LEANING ON THE EVERLASTING ARMS

A. J. Showalter got the inspiration to write this hymn shortly after receiving letters from two friends who had both lost their wives. Writing to express his sympathy, he quoted the scripture passage, "The eternal God is thy refuge, and underneath are the everlasting arms." As he meditated on this passage, it occurred to him that it would make a good basis for a hymn. He then wrote the music and the words of the chorus. He asked a friend of his, Elisha A. Hoffman, to write the verses.

This hymn was first published in its complete form in a hymnal called *The Glad Evangel*, by A. J. Showalter and Co. in 1887.

The simple fingerstyle arrangement is very straightforward and should present no great technical difficulties. The advanced arrangement was inspired by a country band that I heard playing on an old record. It is a virtuoso theme-and-variation type piece.

Melody-only version: Page 243

LEANING ON THE EVERLASTING ARMS

Arranged for the guitar by
Gerard Garno

by Anthony J. Showalter

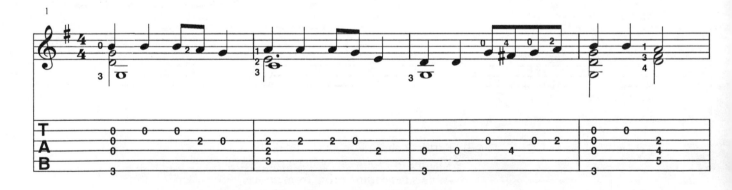

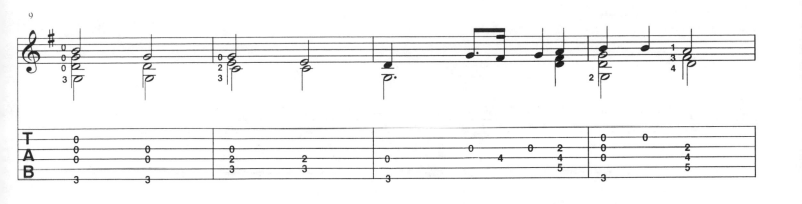

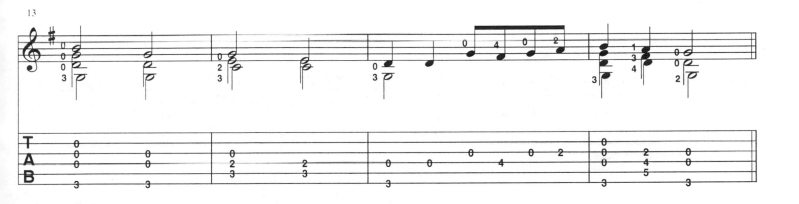

LEANING ON THE EVERLASTING ARMS

Arranged for the guitar by
Gerard Garno

by Anthony J. Showalter

♩ = 108 - 112

6th to D

239

LEANING ON THE EVERLASTING ARMS

Arranged for the guitar
by Gerard Garno

Words by Elisha A. Hoffman
Music by Anthony J. Showalter

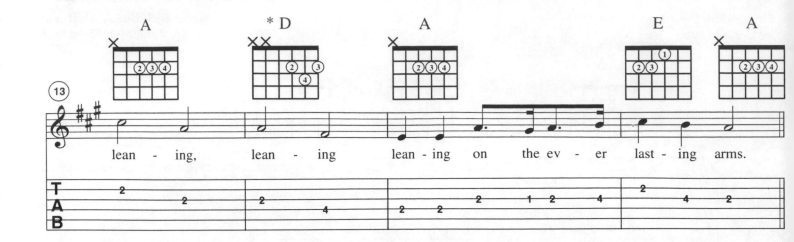

lean - ing, lean - ing lean - ing on the ev - er last - ing arms.

2. O how sweet to walk in this pilgrim way,
Leaning on the everlasting arms.
O how bright the path grows from day to day,
Leaning on the everlasting arms.
Chorus

3. What have I to dread, what have I to fear,
Leaning on the everlasting arms?
I have blessed peace with my Lord so near,
Leaning on the everlasting arms.
Chorus

Greensleeves

(What Child is This)

Old English

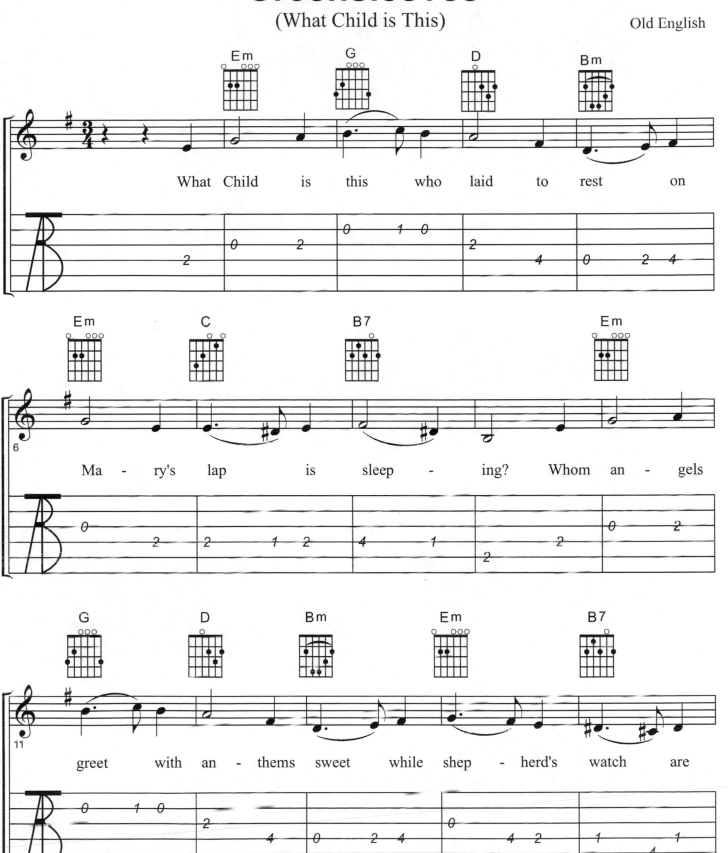

Greensleeves

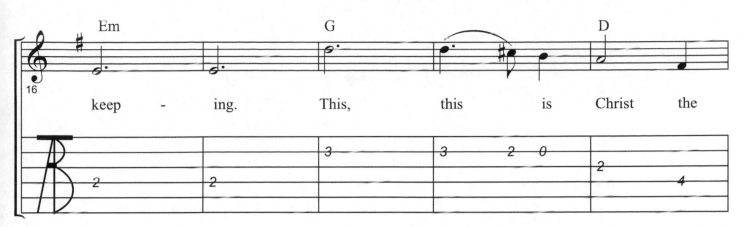

keep - ing.   This,   this   is   Christ   the

King   whom   shep - herds   guard   and   an - gels   sing.

Haste,   haste,   to   bring   him   laud,   the   Babe   the

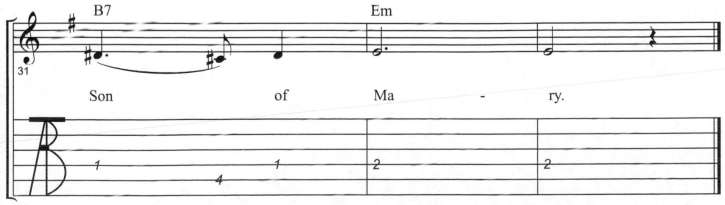

Son   of   Ma - ry.

2

Greensleeves

(What Child is This)

Old English

Greenslecves

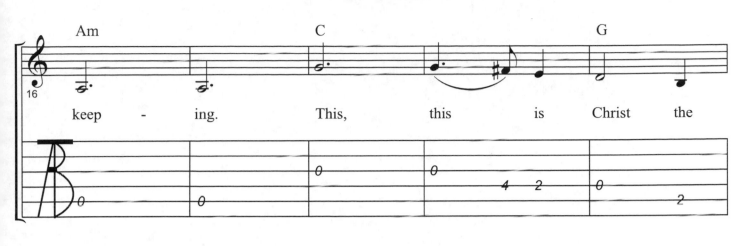

keep - ing. This, this is Christ the

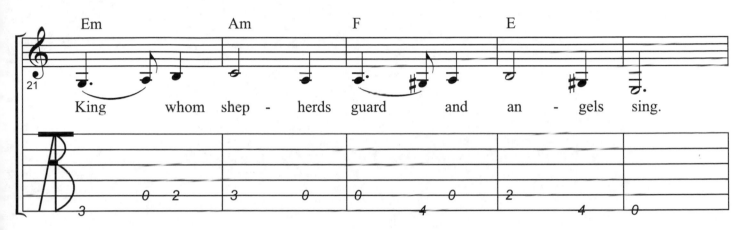

King whom shep - herds guard and an - gels sing.

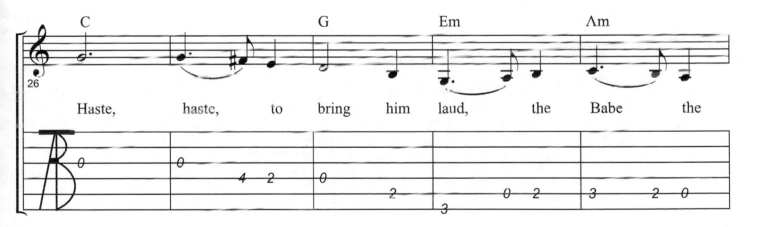

Haste, haste, to bring him laud, the Babe the

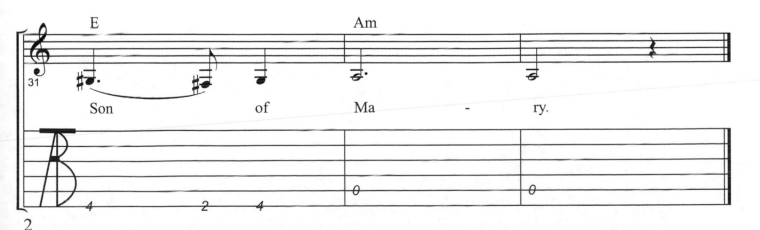

Son of Ma - ry.

2

Greensleeves

www.guitarchordsmagic.com

Visit www.guitarchordsmagic.com for more sheet music and guitar tabs.

Greensleeves

Gently

Annonymous

Chris Peterson ~ CPMusic
www.cpmusic.com

Carolyn Ambuter's Complete Book of Needlepoint

Carolyn Ambuter's
Complete Book of
Needlepoint

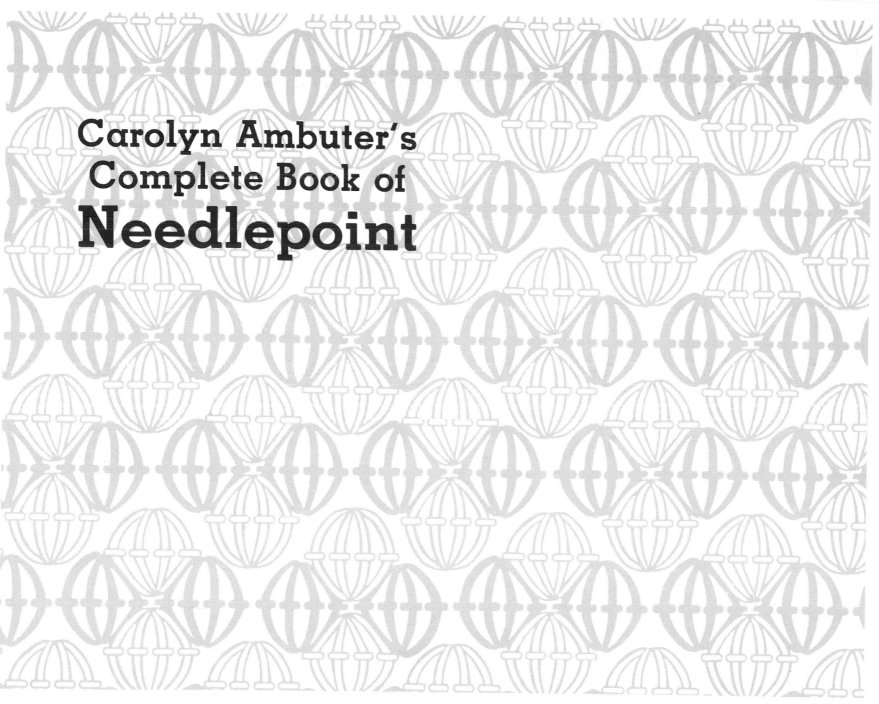